BABES IN THE
MAGIC WOOD
A Family Musical

Book, music and lyrics by
DAVID WOOD

SAMUEL   FRENCH

LONDON

NEW YORK SYDNEY TORONTO HOLLYWOOD

BABES IN THE MAGIC WOOD

First produced at the Queens Theatre, Hornchurch, on the 11th December 1978, with the following cast of characters:

Simple Simon	Richard Albrecht
Contrary Mary	Pauline Siddle
Fairy Godmother/Superwitch	Valerie Minifie
Widow Crockett	Brian Hewlett
Pick	Robert Meadwell
Nick	John Aston
The Donkey	Penny Jones
	Michael Packer
Jack-in-the-Box	Ken Robertson
Ragdoll	Octavia Whitmore
Clockwork Panda	Derek Hewitson
Supermog	
The Vicar	Graham Hoadley
Father Christmas	
Citizens	Roger Hendry
	Lindsay Peters
	Sarah Woodside

(Note: The Citizens can be doubled with other characters)

The play directed by Paul Tomlinson

Settings by David Knapman

PROLOGUE		A grassy bank
ACT I	Scene 1	Town Square
	Scene 2	Inside Widow Crockett's Toyshop
	Scene 3	Town Square
	Scene 4	Inside Widow Crockett's Toyshop
	Scene 5	Mimed silhouette
	Scene 6	Outside the Town
		Transformation to the Magic Wood
ACT II	Scene 1	The Magic Wood
	Scene 2	The Glade of the Walking Trees
	Scene 3	Outside Superwitch's Supercottage
	Scene 4	Inside Superwitch's Supercottage
	Scene 5	The Sky
	Scene 6	Inside Widow Crockett's Toyshop
FINALE		Outside Widow Crockett's Toyshop

CHARACTERS

Widow Crockett	traditional lovable 'Dame' character; she runs a toyshop with her son and daughter.
Simple Simon **Contrary Mary** }	the 'Babes'; he is appealingly ineffectual; she is impetuous and fearless, but never wilful.
Jack-in-the-Box	a bouncy toy, made of springs and things.
Ragdoll	a recognizable doll stuffed with old rags which make her limbs pliable and movement floppy.
Clockwork Panda	toy panda with key in its back; can 'talk' in teddy bear-type noises by pressing · its tummy.
A Donkey	(played by two people) mute but for braying!
Pick **Nick** }	the Robbers, traditionally one stupid and one dominating.
Fairy Godmother/Superwitch	A Fairy Godmother, dressed in black, who turns into Superwitch, entirely dressed in white, with white flashing broomstick. Evil child-eating super yet traditional villainess.
Super Mog	her white cat.
Father Christmas	traditional image.
Superdog	a very brief appearance (seconds not minutes) of a yapping white dog. Could be a real dog or a toy.

Vicar/Carol Singers/Shoppers.

A cast of twelve is ample, various cast members doubling as Carol Singers/Shoppers at the beginning.

SUPERDOG appears very briefly and could be doubled with *FATHER CHRISTMAS*, or be played by a child or A.S.M., or by a real dog, or by a toy.

FATHER CHRISTMAS, only appears at the end. He could be doubled by *SUPERMOG*.

PROLOGUE

A small area downstage. Snow is falling. Music. On a grassy tuffet, Simple Simon and Contrary Mary are curled up asleep. A picnic basket and the remains of a picnic lie beside them. This opening picture resembles the traditional image of the Babes in the Wood. Simple Simon turns over or stretches in his sleep, and rolls off the tuffet, waking up with a bump at the bottom. He sits wide-eyed, takes stock of his surroundings, shudders at the sight of the snow, then jumps up, runs to Contrary Mary and shakes her awake

Simple Simon Hey. Wake up, Mary.
Contrary Mary (*sleepily*) Mmm?
Simple Simon It's late. And it's snowing. We'd better get home.
Contrary Mary (*yawning*) I don't want to go home.
Simple Simon Come on. Mother will be worried. (*He pulls her to her feet and grabs the picnic things.*)
Contrary Mary (*still half-asleep*) I don't want to go home.

They start off, but stop again. Simple Simon looks in the other direction. And back again

Simple Simon Which way did we come? Everywhere looks the same in the snow. Which way's home?
Contrary Mary I don't want to go home.

There is a sudden flash and an eerie, loud noise. Simple Simon and Contrary Mary jump

> *Through the gloom enters a Figure clad in Black—mysterious and rather frightening*

I want to go home. (*She clings on to Simple Simon.*)

They back away as the Figure in Black approaches

Simple Simon Wh—who are you?
Figure in Black Hallo Simon, hallo Mary.
Contrary Mary She knows our names!
Simple Simon }
Contrary Mary } Aaaah! { *speaking*
{ *together*
Figure in Black (*advancing*) Don't be frightened.
Simple Simon She's coming closer!
Simple Simon }
Contrary Mary } Aaaah! { *speaking*
{ *together*
They cling to each other, shaking

Figure in Black I am your Fairy Godmother.
Simple Simon }
Contrary Mary } (*caught up in the rhythm*) She's our Fairy Godmother. Aaaah! { *speaking*
{ *together*

There is a sudden change of mood as they realize

Simple Simon What?
Contrary Mary Who?

The Figure in Black produces a magic wand. The music echoes the amazement of the children. The Lights brighten. A follow spot flashes on the Fairy God-mother. The Children are dazzled

Contrary Mary Why are you here?
Fairy Godmother Why are *you* here?
Simple Simon We're lost.
Fairy Godmother That's why *I'm* here. To get you out of trouble. (*She outstretches her arm*) Come on. I'll lead you home.

Pause. The Children are not sure what to do: but, almost mesmerized, they go to the Fairy Godmother, and exit with her

Music, as the scene changes

ACT I

SCENE 1

The Town Square

Ideally, the first glimpse of this is through the gauze front cloth. Dusk. Snow falling. Traditional Christmas scene. Carol Singers under their lantern. The Vicar conducts. Christmas Tree with lights

Various buildings can be seen in The Square, but the only practical one is the toyshop—"Widow Crockett and Daughter and Son". This has the appearance of a toy house—maybe made of coloured bricks. It is the only building of its kind in The Square—colourful and inviting

SONG 1 **Christmas is Coming**

All   Christmas is coming
The goose is getting fat
Please put a penny
In the hat
If you haven't got a penny
A halfpenny will do
If you haven't got a halfpenny
God bless you.

Christmas is coming
The goose is getting fat
Please put a penny
In the hat.

The singing continues to "Ah..."

The Vicar accepts coins in his hat from passers-by, smiling benevolently and wishing them "Merry Christmas". As the song ends, he goes to the door of the toyshop and rings the bell. The music continues until the door opens

  Widow Crockett emerges

Widow Crockett I've been worried sick. You're a very very naughty boy and I'm very very vexed with you. Take that.

With lightening speed Widow Crockett grabs the Vicar, bends him over and spanks his bottom

Vicar Widow Crockett! Widow Crockett, please! Put me down.

Widow Crockett realises her mistake, stands the Vicar up again and dusts him all over, falling to her knees in mortification

Widow Crockett Oh dear. Forgive me, your relevance—your revelation— your revolting—I mean, Vicar. Forgive me.

Vicar (*backing away*) Of course, of course.

As the Vicar edges back to his amused Carol Singers, Widow Crockett, dusting him to the last, ends up prostrate on the ground

Widow Crockett I mistook you for my Sime Sumple Sinnon, I mean my son Simple Simon. He and his sister Contrary Mary are late home and I've been so worried and—(*Lying flat out, she suddenly becomes aware of the Audience. She witters to a halt*)—and ... (*To the Audience*) Hallo!

Audience participation

Hallo! (*as she gets up, she does a coy wave through her legs*) Hallo–o! I'm Widow Crockett. I expect you know who *you* are! Merry Christmas. This is my toyshop. We make every toy you can think of—from Noah's Arks to knitting kits, xylophones to zebras, Wendy houses to water wings, catapults to Kung Fu costumes, you name it we make it. Of course, Christmas is our busiest time, making presents for all the children ... (*Remembering*) That reminds me, you haven't seen *my* children have you? They're late back and we've so much to do. You'd easily recognize them—one's a girl and one's a boy! Have you seen them?

Audience Yes!

Widow Crockett What were they doing? Where are they?

She gets the audience to mention the Fairy Godmother

Fairy Godmother?

Audience Yes!

Widow Crockett There's no such thing!

Audience Yes, there is, etc.

Widow Crockett Oh, no there isn't!

Audience Oh, yes there is!

Widow Crockett Oh, no there isn't!

Audience Oh, yes there is!

Widow Crockett Oh, no...

Music interrupts her

The Fairy Godmother enters with Simple Simon and Contrary Mary. They stay to one side of the stage—in bright lighting

The following scene is played in a stylized almost dreamlike way, with music throughout

Fairy Godmother Home.

Simple Simon Thank you, Fairy Godmother.

Fairy Godmother (*handing them a bag of what could be sweets*) Here you are.

Contrary Mary What are they?

Fairy Godmother Just a present. Good-bye, now.

Simple Simon } Good-bye, Fairy Godmother. } *speaking*
Contrary Mary } } *together*

Fairy Godmother (*more than just a pleasantry*) I'll see you again soon.

The Fairy Godmother exits

The Lights return to normal. The Children go towards the toyshop. Widow Crockett watches

Widow Crockett (*as they reach the door*) Halt!

The Children stop in surprise

How many times have I told you not to stay out late?

Simple Simon } Sorry, Mother. { *speaking*
Contrary Mary } { *together*

Widow Crockett How many times have I told you not to talk to strange people?

Simple Simon } But... { *speaking*
Contrary Mary } { *together*

Widow Crockett How many times have I told you never to accept sweets from strange people? (*She snatches the "sweets" away*)

Contrary Mary But she's not a strange person.

Widow Crockett She didn't look normal to me.

Simple Simon She's our Fairy Godmother.

Widow Crockett Rubbish. There are no such things as Fairy Godmothers. There are no such things as *fairies*.

Contrary Mary There are.

Widow Crockett Don't be contrary, Mary. Your Mother's never wrong. (*Opening the bag*) Huh. These are fairy *cakes*, I s'pose?

Simple Simon (*looking in the bag*) No, look—they're conkers.

Contrary Mary *White* conkers.

Widow Crockett Useless, whatever they are. Can't even eat them.

Simple Simon They could be *magic* conkers.

Widow Crockett I'll give you a magic conker on the head in a minute. (*Her anger goes—she is really relieved they are back. She puts her arms round them*) Oh, I'm sorry, children. You believe they're magic conkers if you want to. I'm a silly old woman. But I do love you, so I worry about you when you stay out late. See?

They nod

Come on! We can't hang around out here all night. Open the shop, Simon; get ready to serve the customers, Mary.

Simple Simon and Contrary Mary go to the shop

(*Calling after them*) And then we've got to work like stink to finish Father Christmas's order in time. (*To the Audience*) You see...

SONG 2 **By Appointment to Father Christmas**

During the song, customers collect their toys and presents from the Crockett family

One exciting day
Father Christmas came to say
He'd heard the toys we made
Made the grade

Contrary Mary
Simple Simon }   Made the grade

Widow Crockett
Contrary Mary
Simple Simon }   They were the finest toys he'd seen
So ever since we've been—

By appointment to Father Christmas
Suppliers of the highest quality toys
By appointment to Father Christmas
Perfect Christmas gifts
For girls and boys

Passers-by and Carol Singers join in

All   By appointment to Father Christmas
Suppliers of the highest quality toys
By appointment to Father Christmas
Perfect Christmas gifts
For girls and boys.

The lines of this and the next verse can be divided up to individuals if required

Teddies and Teasets
Penny Whistles and Bricks
Skittles and Skateboards
Jigsaw Puzzles and Tricks
Pencils, Stencils
Yoyos and Trikes
Kaleidoscopes
And Skipping Ropes
Money Boxes and Bikes.

By appointment to Father Christmas
Suppliers of the highest quality toys
By appointment to Father Christmas
Perfect Christmas gifts
For girls and boys.

Puppets and Popguns
Kites and Lorries and Trucks
Marbles and Stinkbombs
Rubber Spiders and Ducks
Rocking Horses
Crayons and Chalk
And Model Trains
And Aeroplanes
Dolls that walk and that talk.

By appointment to Father Christmas
Suppliers of the highest quality toys
By appointment to Father Christmas
Perfect Christmas gifts

> For girls and boys.
> Perfect Christmas gifts
> Perfect Christmas gifts
> Perfect Christmas gifts
> For girls and boys.

Pick and Nick enter looking eagerly at the big parcels, etc., being carried off by the shoppers

The last shopper collects a parcel from Widow Crockett at the Toyshop door

Widow Crockett There you are, sir. Merry Christmas.
Customer Thank you.

Pick nudges Nick to try and get a parcel in the same way. Nick stands where the Customer stood. Widow Crockett comes out and gives him a parcel

Widow Crockett There you are, sir. Merry Christmas.
Nick Thank you.
Widow Crockett (*suddenly*) Wait! I don't think we've met.
Nick Oh. Sorry. How do you do?

Nick goes to shake hands, dropping the parcel on Widow Crockett's foot

Widow Crockett Ow!—do you do?
Nick I'm Nick.
Widow Crockett Huh. Nick by name, nick by nature, eh? Trying to nick somebody's Christmas present. This isn't yours.
Nick I—er . . .

Pick approaches—coming to the rescue of Nick

Pick Forgive him, dear lady, a foolish error.
Widow Crockett Who are you?
Pick The name is Pick. (*He overdoes his gracious behaviour, bowing and smiling unctuously*)
Widow Crockett Pick? What do you pick? Pockets, padlocks or noses?

Widow Crockett laughs. Pick laughs. Nick laughs. Pick hits Nick. Nick stops laughing

Pick As I was saying, dear lady, Nick picked up this parcel by mistake. You're so thick, Nick.
Widow Crockett (*suspiciously*) By mistake?
Pick Yes, dear lady. You see—(*Improvizing*)—he is—er—so used to—er—carrying things. We are—er—(*Inspiration*)—furniture removers. We remove your furniture.
Widow Crockett Well, I don't want you to remove *my* furniture.
Nick We remove your furniture whether you want us to or not.

Pick hits Nick. Nick stifles a shriek of pain

Pick Shut up.
Widow Crockett I beg your pardon?

Pick Nothing, dear lady. I was merely remarking to my colleague that you were probably about to—shut up—shop.

Widow Crockett Yes, I am. Extra carefully with you two about. I don't like thieves.

Pick and Nick start to remonstrate

All right. Furniture removers. But whatever you are, you're crooked as a hairpin.

Contrary Mary (*off*) Mother!

Widow Crockett Coming, dear.

Contrary Mary (*off*) Who are you talking to?

Widow Crockett A dirty pair of nickers! (*To Pick and Nick*) Clear off!

Widow Crockett picks up the parcel and goes inside, slamming the door

Pick kicks Nick

Pick You make me sick, Nick.

Nick There's no need to give me a kick, Pick.

Pick I'm hungry. Get the picnic, Nick.

Nick The picnic, Pick?

Pick The picnic, Nick. Quick.

Nick runs to the side, grabs a rope and, to "Yo Heave Ho" music, heaves on the rope. He crosses the stage and exits pulling. Pick grabs the rope at the side Nick entered, and pulls. As he reaches the other side, a Donkey appears, tied on the end. Nick is pushing the Donkey from behind—having dashed backstage to get round again

Although the Donkey is "dumb", he can neigh or whinny occasionally—though this should not be overdone

Nick Giddy up, giddy up. Whoa!

Pick stops pulling, but the Donkey carries on walking

Whoa!

Nick stops. The Donkey continues. Nick falls to the ground

Aaaah! Whoaaaaaaa!

The Donkey walks on and bangs into Pick, who still has the rope over his shoulder. He falls over

Pick Aaaah! (*He gets up, furious*)

The Donkey "poses" for applause

You did that deliberately, you dastardly dangerous dumb donkey. Pass me the stick, Nick.

Nick The stick, Pick?

Pick The stick, Nick. Quick. I'll show him who's master. Ha, ha, ha. (*He tries out a few imaginary strokes*)

The stick is attached to one of the Donkey's saddle bags—round the far side

   It's round here.

As Nick tries to get the stick, the Donkey circles on the spot—keeping the stick out of reach on the far side. This makes Nick circle too

   Stand still. Stop it. Whoa! etc.

After a few circles the Donkey knocks Nick over

   You clumsy, clodhopping, clip clopper.

Pick starts to stand, but exposes his rear to the Donkey, who neatly kicks him down again then poses for applause

   (*Quickly grabbing the stick*) Listen here, Big Ears. One more trick, feel my stick.

Pick threatens the Donkey, who recoils. The audience should by now be ready to boo any anti-Donkey behaviour

   (*Making a loop in the middle of the Donkey rope, and slipping it over a post or part of a fence attached to the toyshop, leaving the other end of the rope still extending off*) Where's that picnic, Nick?
Nick Picnic, Pick
Pick Picnic, Nick.
Nick ⎫ Quick. ⎧ *speaking*
Pick ⎭   ⎩ *together*
Nick It's round here.

Nick goes to a saddle bag. Again the Donkey circles

Pick (*raising the stick*) A—a—a—watch it! If not, feel it! Ha, ha, ha.

The Donkey stops. Nick gets out the picnic

Nick What about him?
Pick What about him?
Nick Shall I give him some picnic, Pick?
Pick Certainly not. He can go without.
Nick But he went without yesterday. And the day before.
Pick You're so thick, Nick.
Nick Thick, Pick?
Pick Thick as a brick, Nick.
Nick A brick, Pick?
Pick A brick ... Oh, shut up and listen.

They sit downstage. Nick unwraps their picnic

Nick My ears are pricked, Pick.

Pick gives him a look. Nick gives Pick a sandwich and takes one himself. They do not eat yet

Pick The point I am making is that the less food we give that quarrelsome quadruped, the less energy he'll have for his stupid pranks.

The Donkey, unseen by them, slowly advances on Pick and Nick

That's log—ic, Nick.

Nick Log—ic, Pick. We'll give him no food at all. Not one mouthful. Not one bite.

As he talks, Nick holds his sandwich in a position such that the Donkey can steal it and eat it. He bows. Nick, turned towards Pick, does not see him, but goes to take a bite. He bites his finger

Ow!

Pick (*turning to him*) What?

Nick I bit my finger.

Pick Twit.

Nick My sandwich disappeared. Have you got it?

Pick 'Course not. This one's mine. So we're agreed, then?

Nick Eh?

Pick We starve the donkey. Starve him till his ribs stick out. Ha, ha, ha.

Nick Ha, ha, ha. Then tickle 'em!

Pick Ha, ha. Tickle his ribs. Ha, ha, ha.

Pick holds his uneaten sandwich out in a position such that the Donkey can pinch it and eat it. He does so, and bows. Pick, still roaring with laughter, goes to eat his sandwich, but bites his finger

Ow!

Nick What?

Pick I bit my finger.

Nick Snap.

Pick Where's my sandwich? (*with sudden fury*) Have you nicked it, Nick?

Nick Nicked it, Pick?

Pick grabs Nick, stand him up, and backs him away, threatening him with the stick

Pick Give it back. (*furiously*) It was my favourite. Chocolate spread and cucumber.

Nick I haven't nicked it, Pick.

The Donkey, seeing that Pick and Nick have moved from the picnic area, moves in and scoffs the remaining sandwiches

Pick Where is it? Give it back, etc.

Pick tries to search the squirming Nick's pockets. Meanwhile the Donkey eats happily. Eventually Pick and Nick see this and stop fighting. Furious, they start creeping up on the Donkey. The Audience will probably shout out a warning. Pick raises the stick

You miserable thieving apology for a horse. Take that. And that. And that.

Pick strikes blows that miss because the Donkey avoids them. Nick tries to steady him. Music

Simple Simon and Contrary Mary rush out of the toyshop and fight off Pick and Nick, using toy swords

A short routine follows, during which Pick and Nick are attacked by Simple Simon and Contrary Mary. They back into wooden sword points, etc., and are attacked by the Donkey with well-aimed kicks. There is a short mini-chase, between the Donkey's legs, etc

  Eventually Nick and Pick run off in defeat

Cheers. Simple Simon and Contrary Mary stroke the Donkey

Contrary Mary It's all right, Donkey, they won't come back in a hurry. (*She removes the rope noose from round the Donkey's neck*)

The Donkey nuzzles their faces

Simple Simon Hey, he's blowing down my ear.
Contrary Mary He's saying thank you.
Simple Simon Oh. (*He blows in the Donkey's ear*)
Contrary Mary What are you doing?
Simple Simon Saying don't mention it.

Widow Crockett's voice calls from the house

Widow Crockett (*off*) Simon. Mary.
Contrary Mary Quick. Hide, Donkey.

Simple Simon and Contrary Mary stand in front of the Donkey, who squats a little

  Widow Crockett enters

The Donkey's position conceals him from Widow Crockett

Widow Crockett (*very quickly*) There you are. I take my eyes off you for a fraction of a second and you're off again leaving me to cope and there's oodles of work to be done and only me to do it and it's not fair. I work my fingers to the bone to keep house and home together and what do I get from you two children? Nothing, that's what I get, nothing. You ought to be ashamed of yourselves for making your poor old mother so unhappy. Boo hoo hoo hoo.

The Children start to speak

And it's no use trying to get round me. It won't wash. You're selfish and ungrateful and I can't take any more, do you hear, I can't take any more, I'm at the end of my tether, I've had enough. Boo hoo hoo hoo. (*She blows her nose very loud to mark the end of this virtuoso complaint*)
Simple Simon (*calmly*) I think we've done something to upset her.
Widow Crockett It's what you *haven't* done that's upset me. All that work for Father Christmas...
Contrary Mary Sorry, Mother. We've got a present for you—a surprise.
Widow Crockett (*softening*) A surprise? Nice or nasty?
Contrary Mary We think it's nice. Close your eyes.
Widow Crockett Ooh. What can it be? (*She closes her eyes*) A magnum of Guinness?
Simple Simon No.
Widow Crockett The latest Boomtown Rats Album? (*Or any current pop idols*)

Simple Simon and Contrary Mary bring the Donkey closer

Simple Simon No.

Contrary Mary puts Widow Crockett's hand on the Donkey's mane

Widow Crockett Ah! A secondhand fur coat! You shouldn't have...
Contrary Mary No.

The Donkey nuzzles against Widow Crockett. She giggles

Widow Crockett It's not the milkman, is it?
Contrary Mary No. Open your eyes.

Widow Crockett does so

Widow Crockett Aaaaaah! (*She faints into Simple Simon's arms*)
Contrary Mary (*to her immobile mother*) Oh Mother, let us keep him. His masters beat him.
Widow Crockett (*coming to*) No, no, send him home.
Simple Simon He hasn't got a home. Have you?

The Donkey shakes his head in an appealingly forlorn manner. At the same time, he neighs—giving the impression that he is answering the question, "nay"

Contrary Mary Aaaaaah.
Widow Crockett But—oh, I don't know. (*To the Audience*) What do you think? Shall we keep him?
Audience Yes!
Widow Crockett Really?
Audience Yes!
Widow Crockett (*shaking her head*) Well—well—well—well ... (*Nodding*) All right, then.

Simple Simon and Contrary Mary cheer

What's your name, Donkey?

The Donkey shakes his head, and neighs/"nays"

Contrary Mary He hasn't got one.
Widow Crockett Well, we can't keep him if he hasn't got a name. He'd never come when we called him.

The Donkey indicates the Audience

Simple Simon What? He's pointing to them.
Contrary Mary I know; he thinks they might be able to think of a good name for him.
Widow Crockett Oh? Well, I wonder ... (*To the Audience*) Can you?

Names are sought from the Audience, and one eventually chosen. Here we will call him "Arthur", but in each performance a different name may be used

Arthur! He likes "Arthur".

Widow Crockett picks up the stick which the Robbers dropped, and rests it on Arthur's back. At first, Arthur recoils, but realizes he is not being hit. Music

I name this donkey Arthur. May God bless him and all who ride on him!

SONG 3 **Don't Say Neigh**

Widow Crockett ⎫	Arthur!
Simple Simon ⎬	Clip clip clippetty clop
Contrary Mary ⎭	Arthur!
	Come and live in our shop
	Arthur!
	We invite you to stay
	Arthur!
	Don't say neigh!
	Arthur!
	Clip clip clippetty clop ...

Widow Crockett Sto——p! (*Indicating the Audience*) They chose the name "Arthur". I reckon they should join in and *sing* the name "Arthur".

Simple Simon and Contrary Mary nod agreement

Will you do that?

Audience Yes!

Widow Crockett (*showing the stick*) Right. I'll conduct you. Whenever the name "Arthur" crops up in the song, belt it out as loud as you can. Make Arthur feel he's among animal lovers. After eight. One, two, three, eight—

SONG 3 **Don't Say Neigh** (*continued*)

All and Audience	Arthur!
All	Clip clip clippetty clop
All and Audience	Arthur!
All	Come and live in our shop
All and Audience	Arthur!
All	We invite you to stay
All and Audience	Arthur!
All	Don't say neigh!
Contrary Mary	Simon is a bit of an ass
Simple Simon	Mary's the most stubborn mule you'll meet
Contrary Mary ⎫ **Simple Simon** ⎭	Mother is a bit of a nag
Widow Crockett	So a donkey makes our family complete!
All and Audience	Arthur!
All	Clip clip clippetty clop
All and Audience	Arthur!
All	Come and live in our shop

All and Audience	Arthur!
All	We invite you to stay
All and Audience	Arthur!
All	Don't say neigh!

It is suggested that during the above chorus, various passers-by and Carol Singers drift on and show an interest, and join in

Optional Donkey Dance: *Arthur, alone or with the others, dances a soft shoe or tap routine. Each time the word "Arthur" is reached in the tune, Widow Crockett conducts the Audience to shout it out. The dance leads into a final chorus*

All and Audience	Arthur!
All	Clip clip clippetty clop
All and Audience	Arthur!
All	Come and live in our shop
All and Audience	Arthur!
All	We invite you to stay
All and Audience	Arthur!
All	Don't say neigh.

Arthur neighs

All (*shouting*)	Don't say neigh!

Towards the end of the song the scene begins to change

SCENE 2

Inside Widow Crockett's Toyshop

If possible the toyshop revolves to reveal the inside. In the main room—the only one we see—there is a chimney, a window, two bunk beds which could fold away when not in use, the front door, another door leading to Widow Crockett's bedroom, work benches, general debris of a toymaker's shop, plus rows of toys; also a large box

> *As song 3 ends, the music continues as Widow Crockett enters the toyshop to start work. The Children lead Arthur off—to stable him. The other passers-by exit. Widow Crockett puts a fancy apron on.*

Optional

Humming the tune of Song 3, Widow Crockett goes behind a work bench—and with a yell falls over, disappearing from view. She clambers up, holding on to the work bench, carrying a skateboard—stepping on this caused her to fall. She looks at it angrily, slams it down, and turns away: But then something draws her back to it. She looks at it, has an idea, checks that the Children aren't coming, and gleefully takes the skateboard and has a go on it. This becomes a virtuoso short "act" of skateboarding, accompanied by "Skater's Waltz"—type of music. She is really enjoying herself

Eventually Simple Simon and Contrary Mary enter through the front door

Widow Crockett collides with them

Contrary Mary Mother, what are you doing?
Widow Crockett Just testing it, dear. Someone has to. Now then—(*she takes up a large, scroll-like list, clearly marked "Father Christmas Order". It unrolls and hits her foot*)—

If the optional scene is not used, Simple Simon and Contrary Mary enter now

They put overalls on

—to work. Mary, sandpaper those jigsaws; I'll sew on teddy bears' eyes; Simon, test those balloons

Widow Crockett gives Simple Simon a packet of balloons. Meanwhile, Contrary Mary gets to work

Simple Simon I've never done that before.
Widow Crockett Just blow them up and check them.
Simple Simon Check them? What for?
Widow Crockett Little holey-woleys.
Simple Simon Little holey-woleys?
Widow Crockett Teeny-weeny little holey-woleys.
Simple Simon Teeny-weeny little holey-woleys?
Widow Crockett Incy-wincy teeny-weeny little holey-woleys.
Simple Simon Incy-wincy...
Widow Crockett Now stop it, Simon. On with the job. (*She returns to work*)

Simple Simon tips out the balloons, chooses one, and with difficulty, blows it up. A drum-roll. He looks pleased, but suddenly lets it go. It whirls up and round and, with luck, into the Audience. He tries again. The same thing happens. He tries again. This time the balloon is a long curly one, which blows up like a catherine wheel—cross-eyed, Simple Simon watches in amazement. By mistake he lets it go—it spins round and round prettily. The next balloon he succeeds in blowing up. He looks at it closely

Simple Simon Any little holey-woleys? Any incy-wincy, teeny-weeny, little holey-woleys? No. Well I'd better put some in!

He suddenly takes a pin and bursts the balloon. He jumps: so do the others

Widow Crockett Simon, what are you doing?
Simple Simon Checking for little holey-woleys. There weren't any so I put one in, and it went off bang.
Widow Crockett Oh you're so simple, Simon. (*Quickly*) When I say blow it up and check for holey-woleys, I mean check there *aren't* any holey-woleys because if there *are* any holey-woleys you won't be able to blow it up. Now get on.

Simple Simon looks confused. He blows up another balloon and ties its neck. He looks at it and calls

Simple Simon I've checked one, Mother. No holey-woleys.
Widow Crockett Well done, dear.
Simple Simon Now what?
Widow Crockett (*patronizingly*) Put it back in the packet.
Simple Simon Right. (*He does a bemused double take as he realizes the implications: big blown up balloon—small packet. He shrugs his shoulders and has a try, contorting himself and the balloon in the process, attempting to stuff it, blown up, into the packet. Grunts of strain*)

Eventually Widow Crockett comes to see what is going on

Widow Crockett What's the matter, dear?
Simple Simon The packet's too small.
Widow Crockett (*imitating*) The packet's too small ... Your brain's too small. Now leave that. We've got to finish this extra special clock. (*She produces a fairly large, bright, colourful clock and holds it up*)

Simple Simon (*putting the balloon debris away*) What's so extra special about it?

He comes round to look, just as a door opens and out pops a grotesque feathered bird. Simple Simon jumps with shock

Bird (*loudly and raucously—possibly over a speaker system, off*) Yoo-hoo!

The bird goes back in and the door shuts. N.B. the mechanism of the clock should be very simple, controllable with one hand

Widow Crockett Did it give you a fright?
Simple Simon No, no. (*He clutches his heart, keels over and faints on the floor. He sits up*) What is it?
Widow Crockett It's a Yoo-hoo Clock. Like a cuckoo-clock but more fun.
Simple Simon (*getting up*) More fun?
Widow Crockett Yes, 'cos you never know when the Yoo-hoo bird is going to pop out.
Simple Simon (*looking closely at the clock*) Really?
Bird (*popping out*) Yoo-hoo.

Simple Simon jumps violently again. The bird pops back

Simple Simon I see what you mean.
Widow Crockett Now, dear, all you have to do is spray the Yoo-hoo bird's feathers. The paint's over there.
Simple Simon Right. (*He collects a can of spray-paint*)
Widow Crockett I'll hold it steady for you. (*She continues to hold the clock, but hides her head behind it*)
Simple Simon Ready.
Widow Crockett Now just concentrate, dear, and the moment he pops out, spray.
Simple Simon Right.

He waits, poised, concentrating. After a few seconds he turns to the Audience and raises his eyes heavenwards as if to say "What a stupid thing to be doing". At that very moment the bird pops out

Bird Yoo-hoo!

Simple Simon jumps violently, turns, goes to spray—but is too late

Widow Crockett Got it, dear?
Simple Simon Not quite, Mother. (*He waits again. Pause. He relaxes a little*) Oh, this is ridic...
Bird (*popping out*) Yoo-hoo!

Simple Simon jumps, turns, goes to spray, but is again too late

Widow Crockett Got it, dear?
Simple Simon Not quite, Mother.
Widow Crockett You're not concentrating.

Simple Simon waits again. Pause. This time he does not move

Bird (*popping out*) Yoo-hoo!

Quick as a flash Simple Simon sprays firmly—but the spray is facing the wrong way, and he only succeeds in spraying his face

Widow Crockett Got it, dear?
Simple Simon Yes, Mother, I got it...
Widow Crockett (*emerging from behind*) Good ... (*seeing him*) Oh! Now come along, Simon. No time to play games. Try again. (*She goes back behind the clock*)

Simple Simon wipes his face, Then waits once more; and waits; and waits. He never moves a muscle

(*Whispering from behind*) Simon.

No reaction

Pssst. Simon.

No reaction

Are you all right, dear?

No reaction

Simon? (*She pops out from behind*) Yoo-hoo!

Simple Simon acts immediately and squirts Widow Crockett's face

Aaaaaaaaah!
Simple Simon Sorry, Mother.
Widow Crockett (*putting the clock on the floor and going to wipe her face*) Never mind. Just wrap it up in nice Christmassy paper.
Simple Simon Right.

Music for a short sequence

1. Simple Simon collects a roll of wrapping paper. He puts it on the floor and unrolls it—but as he unrolls it, it rolls itself up again. He notices this and tries again. The same thing happens
2. He has an idea. He presses one hand on one end of the paper, then unrolls a few feet with the other hand. A good amount of paper is now spread out. He reaches for the clock, and immediately the roll of paper springs closed again
3. He repeats 2
4. A better idea strikes him. He rests one foot on one end of the paper, unrolls a few feet, then plants his other foot on the other end. This involves almost doing the splits
5. He reaches for the clock. At the vital moment it pops open

Bird Yoo-hoo!

Simple Simon jumps and falls flat. He gives up in disgust

Optional routine

Contrary Mary I've finished the jigsaws, Mother.
Widow Crockett Good girl. Now, finish off that toy drum, please. It needs a skin . . .

Contrary Mary fixes the skin and starts testing the drum with a drumstick. The rhythm this provides leads to a funny musical section, depending entirely on the abilities of the actors. Contrary Mary, having established a drum rhythm, Widow Crockett and/or Simple Simon goes into a funny walk, as though taken over by the beat: or they join in a jam session on other toy instruments—e.g. xylophone, toy trumpet, penny whistle, tambourine or kazoo. Whatever the routine is, it is short, and the three characters thoroughly enjoy it. It builds to a climax. At the end, all are breathless, collapsed over benches

  Oh, I enjoyed that. (*She yawns*)
Contrary Mary (*glumly*) We've still got masses to do, Mother. (*She yawns*)
Widow Crockett I know, dear—

Simple Simon snores

  —let's knock off for ten minutes. I'll set the alarm. (*She winds an alarm clock*)

Simple Simon rolls off his bench, falls, and wakes

Simple Simon What's up?
Contrary Mary You're down! We're going to have ten minutes rest, then work all night on Father Christmas's order.
Simple Simon (*yawning*) If only Fairy Godmother would come and help . . .
Widow Crockett I've told you. I don't believe in Fairy Godmothers.
Contrary Mary But wouldn't it be lovely to wake up and find all our work finished—by magic!
Widow Crockett Mmm. But things like that only happen in storybooks.
Simple Simon You never know.
Widow Crockett (*with a smile*) No. You never know.

SONG 4 **If Only**

Simple Simon and Contrary Mary can join in all or part of the song singing a counterpoint to "Ah", if the arrangement provided is not suitable

Widow Crockett   If only
The things we imagine
Could occasionally suddenly come true
If only
Things we only read about in stories
Could happen once in life for me and you
If only
There was such a thing as magic
Just think of all the wondrous spells we'd weave
Maybe the impossible we only dream about
Could be possible
If only
We'd believe.

And the fantasies we make up
Might be real when we wake up
All   If only
We'd just believe.

The music continues

Contrary Mary (*yawning*) If only Fairy Godmother *would* come...
Simple Simon (*yawning*) If only the white conkers were magic...

Simple Simon and Contrary Mary, like Widow Crockett, fall asleep at their benches

Music and lighting tell us something exciting is going to happen—in fact we now go into a dream sequence, which continues for most of the rest of the play. The Audience does not need to realize this yet. As the music grows mysterious, we suddenly become aware of the Fairy Godmother in some unexpected place on the set—maybe up high. With her wand she makes magical passes towards the workshop. The bag of conkers on the workbench magically lights up and appears to pulsate with light—an eerie electronic noise could accompany this

As the focus changes to the flashing conkers, the Fairy Godmother disappears

Suddenly the large box bursts open, and Jack-in-the-Box pops up, swaying and waving about. His clown-like face has a fixed smile, but he does not look frightening. Jack-in-the-Box looks around, then jumps out of his box and bounces—he always jumps or "springs"—over to a pile of toys, or to a cupboard, and reveals Ragdoll. He "wakes her up" and she jerks into life; once or twice she flops and bends, and Jack-in-the-Box straightens her up. The music echoes all this. Together they find Clockwork Panda in another part of the workshop. They wind him up—ratchet noise—using the key in his back. He starts into mechanical movements, and does a short "routine". N.B. It may be possible for Ragdoll and Clockwork Panda to be "on view" from the beginning but it will be a very testing time for the actors involved, since it is very important that the Audience does not see them move until the right moment. So it may be better if they are concealed until Jack-in-the-Box bounces to them. The three Toys mime a conversation gesturing towards the sleeping Widow. All agree what to do

Suddenly lighting and music change to silent-film-style, complete with strobe effect. The three Toys dash round finishing off the work that Widow Crockett and the Children had to do. All of this happens in seconds, at the end of which a tidy pile of perfectly wrapped presents is visible on the workbench, where Simple Simon works

The lighting and music change back as the three Toys congratulate each other, wave farewell and return to their places. Jack-in-the-Box goes inside his box. Ragdoll and Clockwork Panda perhaps remain in view. All three suddenly revert to their lifeless state—taking their cue from the top of Jack-in-the-Box's box slamming shut. Ragdoll flops and Clockwork Panda slows up as if running out of power

The alarm clock goes off with a violent clang. Widow Crockett sleepily gropes for it and turns it off

Widow Crockett Wakey, wakey, children. Rest over.

Simple Simon and Contrary Mary wake up and stretch

   Back to work.

All return to their workbenches. Widow Crockett and Contrary Mary get on with their work. Simple Simon starts yawning mightily. Suddenly he does a huge double take as he sees the finished Toys on the workbench

Simple Simon M-m-m-m-m-mother...
Widow Crockett (*calmly*) Don't dawdle, dear. Get on with your work.
Simple Simon L-l-l-l-l-l-look here...
Widow Crockett *You* look here. Let's all work really hard and we may get finished before Father Christmas comes.
Simple Simon B-b-b-but...
Contrary Mary Oh, shut up, Simon, stop wasting time.
Simple Simon I th-think you *should* l-look, (*To the Audience*) don't you?
Audience Yes!
Widow Crockett Oh, very well. (*She comes over, gives a cursory glance, then starts moving back*) Very nice, dear. (*Suddenly she stops, with a huge gasp. She looks back*)

Contrary Mary, hearing the gasp, turns, looks and reacts too. All stare wide-eyed at the pile of finished toys

   (*After an extended flow of husky, flabbergasted gobbledegook, ending, husky-voiced*) Who did this? (*She coughs. In a very high-pitched voice*) Who did this?
Contrary Mary (*realizing*) Our Fairy Godmother. (*To the Audience*) Right?

Audience Participation

Widow Crockett gets the information from the Audience—i.e., the fact that the Fairy Godmother waved her wand, the conkers lit up and that the Toys finished the Father Christmas order. Contrary Mary and Simple Simon throw in the odd comment—"I knew Fairy Godmother would come back" or "Told you those conkers were magic". When the Audience tell them about the Toys coming to life, they are naturally incredulous—this part of the story is totally new to them. Widow Crockett picks up the scene in the following vein

Widow Crockett (*moving downstage*) You mean they actually came to life?
Audience Yes!
Widow Crockett And finished our work?
Audience Yes!
Simple Simon (*moving downstage*) They couldn't have! You're having us on, aren't you?
Audience No!
Contrary Mary (*moving downstage*) I've never heard of toys coming alive— unless it was real magic. Was it?
Audience Yes.

During the above couple of speeches, the three Toys start coming to life again and advancing on Widow Crockett and her Children. As they get closer, the Audience will probably shout out—"They're behind you", etc. Meanwhile Widow Crockett and the Children shake their heads in disbelief. Suddenly the three Toys approach the three human beings and tap them on the shoulders with three deliberate musically accompanied taps. Widow Crockett and the Children turn, see the Toys and react amazed

Jack-in-the-Box Hallo.
Widow Crockett ⎫
Simple Simon ⎬ Hallo. { *speaking together*
Contrary Mary ⎭
Ragdoll Hallo.
Widow Crockett ⎫
Simple Simon ⎬ Hallo. { *speaking together*
Contrary Mary ⎭
Clockwork Panda (*pressing his stomach, making a noise in the rhythm of "Hallo"*) Grunt grunt.
Widow Crockett ⎫
Simple Simon ⎬ Grunt grunt. { *speaking together*
Contrary Mary ⎭
Widow Crockett (*indicating the Audience*) They were right! You *have* come alive.

The Toys nod

And finished all our work?
Jack-in-the-Box Of course.
Ragdoll Of course.
Clockwork Panda Grunt grunt.

SONG 5 **Toys**

Jack-in-the-Box ⎫   For
Ragdoll ⎬   Your
Clockwork Panda ⎭   Toys
                          Keep you company

When you're all at sea
When you need a friend
For sure your
Toys
Never let you down
Always stick around
Till there's a happy end

Widow Crockett
Simple Simon } It's true
Contrary Mary

All   Your
Toys
Keep you company
When you're all at sea
When you need a friend
For sure your
Toys
Never let you down
Always stick around
Till there's a happy end.

The music continues under the following

Widow Crockett Thank you, toys. We're very grateful. Now, let's see, what sort
of toys are you? (*Taking in the Audience, pointing out Jack-in-the-Box*)
Anyone know what he is?

Audience participation provides the answer

Jack-in-the-Box (*speaking*) That's right. (*He sings*)

I'm
Jack-in-the-Box
Jack-in-the-Box
Bouncing around
On the springs in my socks
If you need me
Give a call
I'll pop out of my box
And help you all.

The music continues under the following

Widow Crockett (*speaking*) Thanks, Jack-in-the-Box. (*to the Audience*) And
who's this? (*She indicates Ragdoll*)

Audience participation provides the answer

Ragdoll (*speaking*) That's right! (*She sings*)

Someone stuffed old rags
In me till I was full

Sewed me a patchwork dress
And made me hair of wool
My limbs are loose and floppy
And I haven't got a brain
But Ragdoll's not too soppy
To help you all again.

The music continues under the following

Widow Crockett Thanks Ragdoll. (*To the Audience*) What about this one?
   (*Indicating Clockwork Panda*)

Audience participation provides the answer

Clockwork Panda grunts an affirmative

Jack-in-the-Box ⎱   He's Panda
Ragdoll ⎰   Clockwork Panda
          You wind him with a key
          He wobbles when he's walking
          And

Clockwork Panda (*pressing his stomach*) Grunts

Jack-in-the-Box ⎱   Instead of talking
Ragdoll ⎰   And sometimes he runs down—

Clockwork Panda's movement slows down jerkily, as does the music

          —As you can see

Jack-in-the-Box winds him up again, till he can move at normal speed

But if you hit a trouble-time
He'll clockwork for you double-time
He's
Clockwork Panda
Never met a grander
Panda
Clockwork Panda.

*Now all three Toy songs are sung together in counterpoint. Jack-in-the-Box sings
his song, Ragdoll sings her song, and Widow Crockett and the Children sing
Clockwork Panda's song*

Following the above, they all sing together

All   For
          Sure
          Your
          Toys
          Keep you company
          When you're all at sea
          When you need a friend
          For sure your

Toys
Never let you down
Always stick around
Till there's a happy end.

Yes
Your
Toys
Keep you company
When you're all at sea
When you need a friend
For sure your
Toys
Never let you down
Always stick around
Till there's a happy end.

At the end of the song, in a short musical coda, the Toys go back to their places, and on the final beat they become lifeless again. The Lights fade to a BLACKOUT

SCENE 3

The Town Square

The Toyshop revolves back to the exterior. It is night, but the scene is not very dark. Street lamps and the lit-up Christmas tree provide sufficient lighting. The donkey rope is still in position, half of it extending off, past the toyshop; a loop fixes it to the fence or some other point, and the other end, to which the Donkey was tied, lies on the ground

Pick and Nick enter, perhaps through the auditorium while the scene change is taking place

Pick (*calling*) Donkey, Donkey!
Nick Donkey, where are you?
Pick It's Picky and Nicky, your ever-loving masters come to take you ho-ome!
Nick (*whistling*) Come on, boy, heel, heel! Come to Nicky and Picky. Puss, puss, puss, I mean donkey, donkey, donkey.
Pick (*losing patience*) Come back here, you mangy mammal, or I'll ...
Nick Here's the square where we had our picnic, Pick.
Pick Where we *didn't* have our picnic, you mean; where that loathsome, ugly, four-legged filcher nicked our picnic, Nick.
Nick Here's his rope. (*He picks up the end which was tied round the Donkey's head*)
Pick Aha! We've got him. (*He removes the loop*) Quick, Pick. Heave.

Music as they heave and strain on the rope, throwing in the odd "Heave", or "Here he comes", or "He'll pay for this". Eventually the end of the rope appears past the toyshop. On it is tied a little toy wooden horse on wheels. Pick and Nick are heaving and straining so hard, eyes closed, that they don't notice this till the toy horse is virtually on top of them. The amount of effort they expend on heaving is totally out of proportion to the ridiculous size of the toy horse

Gotcha!

Suddenly they see the toy horse

Aaaaaah!

Nick (*picking up the horse*) He's shrunk! We shouldn't have starved him!

Pick Don't be so thick, Nick. It's a trick. This is a *toy*. Those horrible toyshop kids who attacked us before—*they* did this. (*Suddenly swinging to the Audience*) Didn't they?

Audience No.

Pick Oh, yes they did.

Audience Oh, no they didn't.

Nick
Pick } Oh, yes they did. { *Speaking together*

Audience Oh, no they didn't.

Nick
Pick } Did. { *Speaking together*

Audience Didn't.

Nick
Pick } Did. { *Speaking together*

Audience Didn't.

Pick They did, 'cos they're kids and all kids are nasty and untrustworthy and evil. (*To Nick*) Look at all that lot.

They survey the Audience

Nick
Pick } Ughhhhh. { *Together*

Pick Wouldn't trust 'em further than I could throw 'em.

Nick
Pick } Ughhhh. { *Together*

Nick Dirty little brats. (*He pokes his tongue out at the Audience*)

By this time, the Audience should love to hate the two Robbers! A sudden loud ringing makes Pick and Nick turn round. Nick drops the horse; Pick drops the rope. They bump into each other, then hide

Widow Crockett pokes her head out of the Toyshop window. She is ringing a large handbell.

Widow Crockett Come on, children. Bedtime.

Simple Simon and Contrary Mary emerge from behind the house

Contrary Mary (*calling*) Good night, Arthur.
Simple Simon Sleep well.

Contrary Mary notices the toy horse on the ground

Contrary Mary Hey, Simon, look. The Robbers must have found it. (*To the Audience*) Have they?
Audience Yes!

Simple Simon laughs

Simple Simon I bet that made them cross!

They laugh. Pick and Nick suddenly emerge in a threatening manner, and advance towards Simple Simon and Contrary Mary. The audience will probably warn the children, who react as if they do not understand. The Robbers get very close, raise their arms to pounce, and do so—but at the last minute, the Children realize what is going on and duck. The Robbers "catch" each other, and grapple away unaware of the fact for a few seconds. Meanwhile Contrary Mary whispers an idea to Simple Simon. They take the rope and stretch it out behind the Robbers. The Robbers, realizing that they are fighting with each other and have missed the Children, stop grappling and turn as if to look for the Children. They trip over the rope and fall headlong

Happily the Children skip into the Toyshop

As the Robbers lie on the ground, Widow Crockett's voice is heard

Widow Crockett (*off*) Right—ready for beddy now. And hurry. Father Christmas will be here to collect his toys soon and he'll be cross if you children aren't far away in the Land of Nod.

Simple Simon (*off*) Eh?

Widow Crockett (*off*) Asleep, Simon, A S L 'eep. Understood?

Contrary Mary (*off*) Yes, Mother.

Widow Crockett (*off*) Leave the toys on the workbench. He'll find them there.

Dramatic chord, as Pick and Nick react and get up

Pick Well, well, well. Father Christmas will be here in a tick, Nick.

Nick (*innocently*) That'll be nice. Maybe we'll get a present.

Pick (*having an idea*) Maybe we *will* get a present—or two ...

Nick Or three. Or four ...

Pick Or more ...

They laugh in anticipation

SONG 6 **The Masters of Crime**

Pick	They've asked for trouble And they're gonna get it!
Nick	They've stolen our donkey But soon they'll regret it
Pick ⎫ **Nick** ⎭	Those kids will pay Pick and Nick will win the day.

We nick a bit here
We nick a bit there
We are the masters of crime
A pilfering pair
With a skill so rare
We've been at it a very long time
We are the masters of crime.

Each Robber tries to deflate the thieving achievements of the other, acting out their stories where appropriate

Nick	I started pinching things
	When I was only three
	At school I pinched the girl
	Who was sitting next to me
	Then I tried some shop-lifting
Pick	He couldn't quite pick it up
	'Cos the shop was far too heavy
	So he dropped it!
Nick	I next became a cat burglar
	And I was brilliant at it
Pick	He stole six hundred cats—but they scratched him
	So he stopped it.

Pick ⎱
Nick ⎰ We nick a bit here
We nick a bit there
We are the masters of crime
It's more than a job
We were born to rob
We've been at it a very long time
We are the masters of crime.

Pick	My story's quite unique
	Though I don't want to boast
	I learned the art of poaching
Nick	You should try his eggs on toast!
Pick	I progressed to dang'rous stuff
	Like blowing up—
Nick	—Balloons?
Pick	No! Safes—
	Till I found the one trick I could
	Really do
	Yes, I became a pickpocket
	The perfect pocket picker
	I don't just steal the contents

He demonstrates on Nick

I steal the pocket too!

He rips off Nick's pocket

Pick ⎱
Nick ⎰ We nick a bit here
We nick a bit there
We are the masters of crime
By hook or by crook
But mainly by crook
We are the masters of crime
You'd better watch out
There are thieves about
A pilfering pair
With a skill so rare

It's more than a job
We were born to rob
We've been at it a very long time
We are the masters of crime.

At the end of the song, Nick and Pick exit, shaking their fists at the Toyshop and the Audience

The Toyshop revolves back to reveal the interior

SCENE 4

Inside Widow Crockett's Toyshop

The Children enter in nightgowns or pyjamas. These costumes might usefully resemble those of Jack-in-the-Box and Ragdoll, though not so obviously that it gives away what happens later. Widow Crockett is pulling out the bunks from the workbenches—it is suggested that two "beds" are built into the workbenches, to save space. They are pulled out like large drawers

Widow Crockett Into bed, you two.

Contrary Mary gets into her bed. Widow Crockett tucks her in.

Simple Simon One, two, hup!

Simple Simon does a spectacular jump on to his bed; as he does so, the bed slides back into the workbench. Simple Simon lands on the floor

Widow Crockett Stop playing, Simon.

Simple Simon tries again—he pulls out the bed

Simple Simon One, two, hup! (*He jumps and again the bed slides in. He lands on the floor*) Ow!
Widow Crockett Simon! (*She places a plate by the hearth*)
Simple Simon I'm sorry, I ... (*As he stands up, the bed shoots out again and knocks him, not over, but on to the bed—this should look almost acrobatic*)
Widow Crockett That's better. Night, Night. I've left Father Christmas his mince pie.

Widow Crockett leaves

Contrary Mary (*tired*) Night.
Simple Simon (*tired*) Night.

The children settle down to sleep. Music establishes "sleep" as the street lamps and Christmas Tree lights in The Square go off, then "tension"

Father Christmas enters through the gloom, "outside" in The Square, tiptoeing carefully. He carries a sack. N.B. It must not be suspected that he is, in fact, an impostor

He stops at the toyshop, goes round behind and climbs carefully in at the window. In the semi-darkness he bumps into a workbench, making a noise. He freezes for a moment; Simple Simon stirs slightly but does not wake up. Father Christmas checks that the Children are asleep, then treads softly towards the presents on the workbench. He starts loading the presents. Contrary Mary sits up in bed, unseen by Father Christmas, watching

Contrary Mary (*suddenly and quite loudly*) Hallo, Father Christmas.

Father Christmas jumps, nearly dropping a parcel

Father Christmas (*in a gruff voice*) Oh, hallo, little girl, you made me jump.
Contrary Mary Would you like a light on? See what you're doing better.
Father Christmas No, no, no. That's quite all right. You should be asleep. You're not meant to see me. (*He goes on filling the sack*)
Contrary Mary Why not?
Father Christmas Well—it's traditional.
Contrary Mary Traditional?
Father Christmas No boy or girl is ever meant to see Father Christmas when he brings them a present.
Contrary Mary But you're not bringing me a present. You're collecting presents.
Father Christmas Oh, well, that's all right then.
Contrary Mary Why are you nervous?
Father Christmas I'm not nervous.
Contrary Mary You're shaking.

Father Christmas drops a parcel, then picks it up. The noise wakes up Simple Simon

Father Christmas I'm old.
Contrary Mary How old?
Simple Simon (*sitting up*) Hallo, Father Christmas!

Father Christmas jumps

Father Christmas Hallo, little boy.
Simple Simon How was the mince pie?
Father Christmas Eh—what?
Simple Simon Don't say you haven't eaten it. (*He goes to look. To Contrary Mary*) He hasn't. (*To Father Christmas*) It was waiting for you. By the fire-place.
Father Christmas Oh, sorry. I didn't see it.
Simple Simon You must have done . . .
Contrary Mary (*with a sudden change of mood*) He didn't see it because he's a cheat. A fraud.
Father Christmas (*nervously*) What do you mean?
Contrary Mary I was awake all the time. You didn't see your mince pie because you didn't come down the chimney like any self-respecting Father Christmas, you came in the window.
Simple Simon (*disgustedly*) The window?
Father Christmas I told you. I'm old. Anyway—

The Children stand and almost menacingly "crowd" him

there aren't so many fireplaces as there used to be—what with central heating ...

A sudden urgent voice off stops all in their tracks.

Pick (*off*) Nick, get a move on.
Contrary Mary Who was that?
Father Christmas (*speaking the line towards the window to warn Pick that things are going badly*) M-m-m-m-my—reindeer. He's waiting outside.
Contrary Mary A talking reindeer?
Father Christmas Why not?
Simple Simon Why did he call you Nick?
Father Christmas (*backing to the window with the sack*) W-w-well. Nick—you know—Saint Nicholas—one of my names—Santa Claus—Saint Nicholas—Old Nick—patron saint of children—now, come on, get out of my way.
Contrary Mary That beard doesn't look real to me, Father Christmas.
Father Christmas Get away, of course it's real ...

Too late. Contrary Mary pulls the beard off revealing Nick, the Robber

Simple Simon It's *him*!
Contrary Mary Get him!

Music, as a mini-chase starts, during which Nick makes a run for it, leaving the sack by the window. Various incidents follow, falling over, etc. at one point, the Children corner Nick. He makes a run between them. A struggle. At this point, Pick appears at the window and, sizing up the situation picks up the sack and lifts it out through the window. Nick's Father Christmas outfit is nearly off. He escapes from the children, rips the coat off and throws it over them. They writhe about under it as he pinches the last couple of parcels—plus, because it's so close, the bag of magic conkers, and Widow Crockett's bell, which is nearby. He throws them out to the waiting Pick, and makes his escape

With evil laughter Nick and Pick cart off the sack through The Square and exit

The Children escape from the Father Christmas coat, rush to the window and see the escaping Robbers

Simple Simon (*in a panic*) What are we going to do? What are we going to do? (*Calling*) Mother, Mother!
Contrary Mary Shut up. Don't panic.
Simple Simon I'm not panicking! I'm not panicking! (*pause, he thinks*) What are we going to do? What are we going to do? They've taken all Father Christmas's toys.... (*He gasps as he notices*) And the magic conkers, too. Mother, Mother!
Contrary Mary Shut up. We mustn't wake up Mother.
Simple Simon Mustn't wake up Mother? When she finds out what's happened, she'll never sleep again.

Arthur suddenly pokes his head in at the window, if possible nudging Simple Simon in the back. Simple Simon jumps

Ahhh! Oh, it's you Arthur. You'll never guess what's happened.

Arthur nods

You *know* what's happened?

Arthur nods

(*panicking again*) Then what are we going to do?

Arthur uses his head to point in the direction in which the Robbers left

What?

Arthur does it again

(*to Contrary Mary*) What's he saying?
Contrary Mary I don't know. (*To the Audience*) Do you know?

The Audience will probably shout out "he's saying 'go after the Robbers'"

Follow them? Get the toys back?
Audience Yes.
Contrary Mary Is that right, Arthur?

Arthur nods

Right. Come on, then, Simon. Arthur, are you coming too?

Arthur nods

Thank you!

SONG 7 **We Gotta Follow**

During the song, Simple Simon and Contrary Mary, who for virtually the rest of the play will be in their night clothes, each grab a sheet from their beds and climb through the window

Simple Simon }
Contrary Mary }   We gotta follow!
                        We gotta follow!
                        We gotta follow!

                        We gotta follow
                        Follow the Robbers
                        Follow the Robbers
                        Who stole the toys.

                        We gotta follow
                        And get the toys back
                        For if we don't
                        Father Christmas's sack
                        Will be empty and
                        Thousands of girls and boys
                        Will wake up on Christmas Day
                        With no toys.

We gotta follow!
We gotta follow!
We gotta follow!

At the end of the song, all exit in pursuit of the Robbers. If possible, Contrary Mary sits astride the Donkey

The music continues

Widow Crockett enters from the door leading to her bedroom. She is in nightie and curlers

Widow Crockett (*crossly*) Children, children. Cease this racket and go to sleep. (*She looks at the empty beds, does not at first register, and turns away muttering*) Disgraceful hoo-ha ... (*A sudden huge double-take swings her back again as she realizes the beds are empty*) Hoo! Ha! (*Building as she realizes they have gone*) Hoo! Ha! Ha! Ha ha ha! Hoo! Children! (*Almost screaming*) Children! They've gone. They've vanished. Aaaaah. (*She sees the open window*) Aaaaah! Where are they?

She gets the information from the Audience that the children are chasing after the Robbers

What, the furniture removers?
Audience Yes.
Widow Crockett What were *they* doing here?
Audience Stealing the toys.
Widow Crockett What? (*She notices that the pile has vanished*) Aaaaah! Father Christmas's special order! (*She takes up a boxer's stance and shadow boxes*) I'll get 'em. I'll show 'em. I'll bash 'em. Take that. And that. And that.

This becomes a short virtuoso funny fight for one—possibly using a workbench and/or a door to achieve effects like a hand grabbing the neck and pulling it out of sight, the head reappearing and being grabbed again—or pulling herself over the workbench and rolling off the other side. In other words, Widow Crockett has a fight but does all the work of her opponent as well. Then suddenly she "wakes up"

Emergency, that's what it is. Emergency! (*A cry from the heart*) Who will help a poor old woman in her hour of need!

The Audience may shout out "Wake up the toys"

(*eventually*) The Toys—Jack-in-the-Box, Ragdoll and Clockwork Panda. They helped us before. (*Singing*) Toys never let you down ... (*To the Audience*) Come on, help me—let's all shout out ...
Toys please come alive
When we've counted up to five ...
All together ...

All Toys please come alive
When we've counted up to five ...

Widow Crockett asks the Audience to do better, if necessary, and shout it again

Widow Crockett (*eventually*) Right, cross your fingers everyone—and count with me . . .

All One, two, three, four, FIVE!

Exhausted by the effort, Widow Crockett leans on the box. Suddenly it springs open, almost knocking her over. There is a short silent film-type sequence— music and strobe lighting

> *In double quick tempo, Jack-in-the-Box appears, gets out of his box and wakes up Ragdoll. Both of them wind up Clockwork Panda, who jerks into life also*

Lighting returns to normal, as all three stand facing Widow Crockett

Jack-in-the-Box How can we help?
Ragdoll How can we help?

Clockwork Panda presses his stomach and grunts in the rhythm of "How can we help?"

Widow Crockett Follow me. Rescue the children!

SONG 7A **We Gotta Follow** (*reprise*)

> *During the song Widow Crockett, possibly grabbing a dressing gown, leads the three Toys out of the door. As soon as they are out, the set begins to move— to suggest movement as they set out off from The Square, and also to prepare for the next scene*

Widow Crockett } We gotta follow!
Jack-in-the-Box } We gotta follow!
Ragdoll } We gotta follow!
(Clockwork Panda) }

We gotta follow
Follow the Children
Follow the Children
Who followed the Robbers
Followed the Robbers
Who stole the toys.

We gotta follow
And get the toys back
For if we don't
Father Christmas's sack
Will be empty and
Thousands of girls and boys
Will wake up on Christmas Day
With no toys.

We gotta follow!
We gotta follow!
We gotta follow!

SCENE 5

A Silhouette Mime

*It is suggested that the stage is virtually empty apart from a cyclorama and maybe
a cut-out shape or two against it. The aim is to re-establish who is chasing after
whom and to do this in an enjoyable, eye-catching manner. It would be effective
if the characters had to negotiate a hazard of some kind—a style, or a chasm
which requires them to swing over on a rope*

The music during the scene echoes the action, silent-film-style

1. *Pick and Nick face the hazard. Their main problem will be how to get the
heavy sack of toys over*
2. *Contrary Mary and Simple Simon with Arthur, the Donkey. Clearly getting
Arthur across could cause problems—and Simple Simon could very well be nervous and have to be encouraged by Contrary Mary*
3. *Widow Crockett and the three Toys. Added fun could be gained here from
Jack-in-the-Box bouncing over the hazard, Ragdoll having to be carried, and
Clockwork Panda running out of juice in the middle—requiring a re-wind, complete with ratchet noise*

SCENE 6

Outside the Town—nowhere in particular

*The set could be a continuation from the previous Scene—a virtually empty stage
with a cyclorama. Lighting suggests moonlight, with the moon visible on the
cyclorama*

> *Pick and Nick enter, Pick leading the way. Nick staggers under the weight
> of the toys*

Pick Quick, Nick.
Nick (*under the weight*) Ohhhhh. Hang on a tick, Pick.

> *Pick crosses back behind Nick to look off and check whether they are being
> followed. Unbeknown to him, Nick stops—facing off in the other direction*

Pick All clear. We'll rest a tick, Nick. (*He turns back and bumps into the sack
on Nick's back*) Aaaah!
Nick Sorry, Pick.
Pick Put it down.

Nick swings the sack round; it hits Pick and knocks him over

> Aaaah!
Nick Sorry, Pick.
Pick (*getting up*) Just drop it.

Nick drops it—on Pick's foot

> Aaaah!
Nick Sorry, Pick.

Pick (*echoing*) Sorry, Pick, sorry, Pick. You really get on my wick, Nick.
Nick Sorry, Pick.
Pick And stop saying "Sorry, Pick".
Nick Sorry, Pick. (*He realizes he has said it*) Oof . . . (*He whispers*) Sorry, Pick.
   (*He repeats the phrase a couple of times, till it whittles away to nothing*)
Pick Now, let's open the sack and look at the loot.
Nick Yes, let's look at the loot.

They move in to the sack and bang heads

Pick
Nick } Ow! { *together*

Pick You open the sack.
Nick No, you open the sack.
Pick You open it.
Nick No, you open it.
Pick After you.
Nick After you.
Pick Please.
Nick Please.

Pick
Nick } Oh, all right, *I'll* open the sack. { *Speaking together*

They move in to the sack and bang heads again

   Ow!

Pick opens the sack, and brings out a parcel

Pick (*pleased*) Oh yes!

Nick brings out another

Nick Oh yes!

Pick brings out another

Pick Oh yes!

Both bring out Widow Crockett's bell and ring it

Pick
Nick } Oyez, Oyez!

Pick Shut up.
Nick Sorry, Pick. (*He realizes he has said it again*) Oof . . .

Pick gives Nick a filthy look. Nick puts the bell back in the sack

Pick We've done well, Nick. Never again will those donkey-thieving kids trick
   Pick and Nick.
Nick We've licked 'em, Pick.
Pick (*relishing the thought*) When the real Father Christmas comes, there'll
   be no toys for him and he'll quiver and quake and shout, "I'll never order
   another toy from this toyshop".
Nick "Never, ever".

Pick (*inciting the Audience to boo*) And Widow Crockett and her two horrible brats will starve!

Nick And rot!

Pick ⎫
              Ha ha ha ha ha! {*together*
Nick ⎭

Pick (*with a change of mood—bringing out the bag of magic conkers*) What's this?

Nick I don't know. It was on the table so I nicked it, Pick.

Pick Load of rubbish. Mouldy old conkers.

They each take a handful. Tension Music

Dump them here.

Nick Maybe they're valuable.

Pick No. Rubbish. Extra weight in the sack. We'll throw them away.

Nick Are you sure?

Pick 'Course I'm sure.

Pick throws his handful away. Music echoes this. Nick shrugs his shoulders and does the same. Immediately eerie electronic music accompanies a strange pulsating light which covers the whole stage—as though the scattered magic conkers are all pulsating and covering the whole area. Pick and Nick react frightened to this and turn to see what on earth is going on

Transformation Scene

Suddenly, as though springing from the conkers, a white wood begins to grow; excitingly-shaped trees rising from the conker seeds. If possible this is orchestrated in such a way that the Robbers are several times taken by surprise by a tree growing near them; they move to "safety" and another grows in the spot to which they have moved. Dry ice could be used to create a magical cotton-wool carpet in the wood. If possible the transformation lasts a minute or two, building gradually rather than all happening at once. The lighting increases too, still pulsating, so that by the final stage of the transformation, the stage is a dazzling white colour. Although "in reality" it is night-time, in the magic wood the trees almost seem to create or reflect light

Pick and Nick watch in fright and fascination. If possible, a few all-white creatures such as bats—flown in or tracked across—swoop in among the trees and brush against the two Robbers

SONG 8 **The Magic Wood**

Pick ⎫   Are we bats?
                                 Are we bonkers?
Nick ⎭   Could this be a dream?

Pick ⎫ Pinch me (*They pinch one another*)   ⎰ *speaking*
Nick ⎭ Aaaaaaah! (*Terrified*) It's *not* a dream! ⎱ *together*

                      (*Singing*) Then could it be
                                      These conkers
                                      Are more than they seem?

> We're walking through a wood
> That we're sure wasn't here
> When we walked this way before
> Could this wood
> Be a magic wood?
> Do you think it's safe to explore?
> Could this wood
> Be a magic wood?
> If it is, what myst'ries lie in store?

Simple Simon and Contrary Mary, with Arthur the Donkey, enter

Pick and Nick weave their way through the trees. They do not exit, but stay visible though unobtrusive. Simple Simon and Contrary Mary react amazed by the wood

Simple Simon ⎫
Contrary Mary ⎬   Did it spring up overnight
(Arthur)   ⎭   Why is it all white?
                        Do you think we'll be all right
                        If we go on?

They weave through the trees

> *Widow Crockett and the three Toys enter, and also react astonished. They are not aware of the other groups*

Widow Crockett   ⎫
Jack-in-the-Box   ⎬   Will we ever find our way?
Ragdoll   ⎬   How long will it stay?
(Clockwork Panda)   ⎭   Will we wake one day
                            And find it gone?

All three groups now sing together. But they remain in their groups and are never aware of the other groups. In other words, there are three lost groups of characters wandering independently through the Magic Wood, but having the same reaction of wonder towards it

All   We're walking through a wood
                            That we're sure wasn't here
                            When we walked this way before
                            Could this wood
                            Be a magic wood?
                            Do you think it's safe to explore
                            Could this wood
                            Be a magic wood?
                            If it is, what myst'ries lie in store?

There follows a short section of fugue/counterpoint, using the chorus in three parts—one part for each group

Group One   We're walking through a wood
                            That we're sure wasn't here
                            When we walked this way before
                            We're walking through the wood
                            Yes, we're walking through the wood

That we're sure wasn't here
When we walked this way before
Will we ever find our way?
How long will it stay?
Will we wake one day
And find it gone?

Group Two   We're walking through a wood
That we're sure wasn't here
When we walked this way before
We're walking through the wood
Yes, we're walking through the wood
That we're sure wasn't here
When we walked this way before
Will we ever find our way?
How long will it stay?
Will we wake one day

Group Three   We're walking through a wood
That we're sure wasn't here
When we walked this way before
We're walking through the wood
Yes, we're walking through the wood
That we're sure wasn't here
When we walked this way before
Will we ever find our way?

All   We're walking through a wood
That we're sure wasn't here
When we walked this way before.

As the song ends, Pick and Nick exit, with their sack. Widow Crockett and the Toys also exit

Simple Simon and Contrary Mary are left, with Arthur the Donkey

Simple Simon   Could this wood
Contrary Mary   Be a magic wood?
If it is, what myst'ries lie in store?
Contrary Mary We've been past this tree before. We're going in circles.
Simple Simon Must be a round trip.
Contrary Mary (*stopping*) Well, I don't know where we are. (*She shakes her head*) Do *you* know where we are?

Arthur neighs/"nays"

He doesn't know where we are.

All three shake their heads

Simple Simon } We're lost! Help! { *Speaking*
Contrary Mary }   { *together*

There is a sudden flash

As if by magic the Fairy Godmother appears—black against the white of the wood

Fairy Godmother Hallo, Simon. Hallo, Mary. Hallo, Arthur.
Simple Simon Fairy Godmother!
Fairy Godmother Welcome to the Magic Wood.
Contrary Mary It *is* a magic wood. I knew it!
Fairy Godmother I said we'd see each other again soon.
Simple Simon We're lost again, Fairy Godmother.
Fairy Godmother No, you're not.
Contrary Mary We are! We're chasing the robbers who stole the toys for Father Christmas and ...
Fairy Godmother I know. But you're not lost. I'm with you. And the robbers aren't far ahead.
Simple Simon But which way did they go?
Fairy Godmother Don't you know? (*Indicating the Audience*) Everyone else does!
Simple Simon Do they? (*To the Audience*) Do you? Which way did they go?

The Audience tells them

Thank you.
Fairy Godmother Off you go, then. That way.
Contrary Mary Thank you, Fairy Godmother. Come on, Arthur.

Simple Simon, Contrary Mary and Arthur run off

The Fairy Godmother waves good-bye

Fairy Godmother Off you go. Off you go. But you'll never come back. Ha, ha, ha, ha, ha.

Cackling horribly, the Fairy Godmother with a flourish discards her black garb, to reveal underneath a traditional witch costume—except that it is all white. She carries a white broomstick, which ideally pulsates with light the way the bag of conkers did. Music echoes her change, which happens as swiftly as possible. Maybe the black cloak is flown, and disappears upward

(*Imperious*) For I am not a Fairy Godmother at all. I am Superwitch!

Chord, or a short send-up of "Superstar" theme

Sophisticated, scientific, spell-monger supreme. Superwitch. And this is my Superwitch's cat—Supermog!

A chord and a flash

Supermog appears as if by magic. He, too, is all white. He hisses and paws the air threateningly

And we hate, loathe and despise—children. Except the occasional one or two—to eat—boiled, scrambled or fried. Thanks to Superwitch's super-powerful superbrain, Simon and Mary will never leave my Magic Wood. They will never see their home or their mother again. (*Cackle, cackle*) Super-witch rules—okay? (*Cackling maniacally she starts to exit*)

During the above, Supermog yawns, stretches, and curls up to go to sleep—a recurring trait in his character is his constant doziness

(*noticing Supermog is asleep*) Supermog!

Supermog wakes with a start and follows her. Ideally, Superwitch gets on her broomstick and flies away. The music builds to a sinister climax, as—

the CURTAIN *falls*

ACT II

SCENE 1

The Magic Wood. Night

If possible, the wood has become slightly thicker—in other words it looks like "another part of the wood"—a deeper part. There is a white log to sit on. The trees are still bright white, but the cyclorama is dark—midnight blue—and the trees cast odd shadows. There is eerie music, and a general spooky atmosphere

Nick and Pick enter, heads down, following the track. Nick leads, carrying the sack of stolen toys over his back

An owl hoots loudly. Nick stops, alarmed. Pick carries on walking and bumps into the sack

Pick Ow! Nick. What have you stopped for?
Nick (*with an eerie tremor*) Didn't you hear it?
Pick What?
Nick The hoot of an owl. Calling me.
Pick Calling you?
Nick Calling me. Toowit toowoo. Toowit toowoo.
Pick Calling you "Twit, you Twit" more like.
Nick You may laugh.
Pick Thank you. Ha, ha, ha.
Nick You may make fun of me.
Pick Thank you. Your face looks like an over-ripe tomato that's been sat on by a hippopotamus.
Nick It's no joke.
Pick I think your face is a big joke.
Nick The hoot of an owl at midnight means that ghostly spirits are roaming abroad.
Pick Well, if they're roaming abroad, they won't bother us, will they?
Nick Abroad—about—everywhere—here—now.
Pick What—ghosts?
Nick I don't know *what* ghosts, just ghosts.
Pick Oh well, if they're *just* ghosts, we've nothing to fear. Anyway ...

SONG 9 **Things That Go Bump in the Night**

Pick
I don't believe in ghosts and spooks
It's all a load of rubbish
That we read in silly books
I don't believe in things that go bump in the night
'Cos nothing supernatural could ever give me a fright.

Nick (*speaking*) Really?

Pick Really.
Nick Nothing shuddery or spine-chilling could ever give you a fright?
Pick Nothing.

Nick (*singing*)	Imagine a haunted house
	And you're opening the door
(*Making the sound*)	Creak, creak
	Suddenly evil laughter
	Echoes from under the floor
(*Making the sound*)	Laughter
	There's a violent screech from a vampire bat
(*Making the sound*)	Screech, screech
	And a bell that tolls, cracked and flat
(*Making the sound*)	Dong, dong, dong, dong
	Then you turn and to your horror
	Through the eerie gloom
	A headless lady is floating through the room.
(*Making a ghostly* *sound*)	Woooahhhh!

Throughout the above Pick remains unmoved and unconcerned

(*speaking*) Well, didn't that frighten you?
Pick Of course not! I told you ...

(*singing*)	I don't believe in ghosts and spooks
	It's all a load of rubbish
	That we read in silly books
	I don't believe in things that go bump in the night
	'Cos nothing supernatural could ever give me a fright.

Pick sits down confidently—turned away from Nick and the Audience. Nick comes forward and speaks to the Audience conspiratorially

Nick (*to the audience in a loud whisper*) Come on, let's see if *you* can frighten him! You do all the spooky, creepy noises with me, all right? Make them really *terrifying*!

(*singing*)	Imagine a haunted house
	And you're opening the door
(with the audience)	Creak, creak
	Suddenly evil laughter
	Echoes from under the floor
(with the audience)	Laughter
	There's a violent screech from a vampire bat
(with the audience)	Screech, screech
	And a bell that tolls, cracked and flat
(with the audience)	Dong, dong, dong, dong
	Then you turn, and to your horror
	Through the eerie gloom
	A headless lady is floating through the room.
(with the audience)	Woooahhhh!

During the above, Pick, back to audience, reacts nervously, until in the end he runs around terrified. The idea is that the Audience is encouraged to make Pick progressively display more and more fright. Nick laughs. Pick suddenly notices the Audience

Pick (*to the Audience*) It was *you*. You horrible horde.
Nick They were taking the mick, Pick.
Pick Grrr. Well, at least there's no sign of that other pair of tricksy kids. Come on, let's have a quick kip, Nick. (*To the Audience*) And you lot, watch it. You won't fool me again. (*Yawning*) I don't believe in ghosts.

Nick and Pick sit or half-lie against the log.

   Sudden tension music, as a Ghost enters from among the trees and approaches the Robbers

The Audience will probably scream—not from a desire to warn the baddies but in anticipation of what will happen when they see it—also for the sheer fun of it. The Ghost advances menacingly on the Robbers, who are asleep. It trails its white shroud over Nick's face, then retreats. His nose twitches, he sneezes, but he goes back to sleep. The Ghost reappears and repeats the tickling. This time Nick sneezes and wakes with a start. The Audience will probably warn Nick of the Ghost behind him. He reacts frightened and walks nervously across the stage followed by the Ghost. In mime, Nick asks the Audience "Is it behind me?" then turns suddenly. The Ghost hides behind a tree in the nick of time. Nick pretends the Audience is playing a joke. This is repeated—Nick walks, Ghost follows, Nick turns, Ghost hides. The third time, Nick turns, Ghost hides, Nick shakes his head—the Ghost appears again and Nick suddenly sees it. Short chase—Nick terrified. Eventually the Ghost disappears behind the trees. Nick dashes to Pick and wakes him up. Pick is cross

Nick A g-g-g-g-g-ghost!
Pick Rubbish!
Nick N-n-n-n-n-no!
Pick Where?

Nick points to the trees. Pick resolutely strides over and wanders among the trees, looking. He emerges shaking his head—after a couple of seconds, the Ghost follows him—inches away from him. Pick comes forward shaking his head etc., to indicate "There is nothing there". Nick and the Audience scream that the Ghost is behind him. The Ghost wafts a "sleeve" of its shroud over Pick's face. He turns to jelly, plucks up courage, turns, sees the Ghost, screams and runs a fair distance as if to exit. The Ghost disappears behind a tree

   Simultaneously another Ghost appears to meet Pick

Pick stops in his tracks, screams, turns back, runs, and meets the first Ghost, who pops out again. A short sequence follows during which the two Robbers are chased by the two Ghosts. The Robbers collide with each other and get in total confusion. This sequence will have to be devised for each production, as it will depend greatly on the positions of the trees. Music accompanies this almost choreographed chase

Finally Pick and Nick escape, with their sack, and exit, wailing

The two Ghosts remain and swiftly remove their shrouds. They are Simple Simon and Contrary Mary, who laugh heartily at the confusion they have caused

Simple Simon They went white as a sheet!
Contrary Mary Good thing we brought *our* sheets with us!
Simple Simon They thought we were real ghosts! Woooah. (*He makes a haunting noise and gesture*).
Contrary Mary Everyone knows there aren't any *real* ghosts.
Simple Simon They're just stupid.
Contrary Mary Not that stupid. They've still got the toys. Come on.

As they start to move, two "real" Ghosts enter and advance from the trees, downstage towards the Children

The Audience will shout a warning.

The Children stop in their tracks down C but do not believe the Audience; they think they are having them on. As if to prove there are no ghosts there, they walk in circles—in opposite directions returning to the same spot. The two Ghosts follow close behind so that the Children do not see them. The Children look at the Audience as if to say "there, we've proved it—there are no Ghosts". Then, with supreme confidence, they turn round to go, and bump straight into the Ghosts, who adopt a haunting posture. In stylized manner the Children turn to face Audience again, eyes wide. In terror they pause, then move—in towards each other and collide, then, pursued by the Ghosts, they run in opposite directions in a large circle and meet and collide upstage

After a short chase through the trees, the Children exit; in the confusion they leave behind their sheets

The two haunting sequences should not be too similar and it is probably best if the second, where the Children see the Ghosts, is shorter than the first. The Audience participation with the Ghosts is likely to veer towards the hysterical so the chases, etc., must be very tightly controlled

The two "real" Ghosts tear off their ghostly garb and reveal themselves as Superwitch and Supermog

Superwitch (*cackling*) Superwitch rules! My super plan is working superbly. Those children are one step nearer their superfate. (*cackle*) Come, Supermog.

During the above, Supermog yawns, stretches and falls asleep

Supermog!

Supermog wakes up

Superwitch and Supermog exit, to sinister music
The music changes to "Donkey" music

Arthur enters, on his own. He looks off, looks behind trees, etc., searching for the Children. If possible, he shrugs his "shoulders" as in each place he looks he draws a blank. He shakes his head, sad

Widow Crockett (*off*) Left, right—

Widow Crockett enters, followed by the three Toys, through the trees

—left, right, left, right—(*She stops to encourage the others. To Jack-in-the-Box*)—bounce, bounce—(*To Ragdoll*)—hop, skip—(*To Clockwork Panda*)—waddle, waddle. Left, right, bounce, bounce, hop, skip, waddle ... (*She sees Arthur*) It's Arthur! Rescue party—halt!

The Toys and Widow Crockett crowd round Arthur, who does not react—just stares gloomily ahead

Hallo, Arthur. Where are the children?

Arthur shakes his head

You don't know?
Jack-in-the-Box (*finding the discarded sheet*) What's this?
Ragdoll (*picking up the other discarded sheet*) What's this?

Clockwork Panda presses his tummy and growls in the rhythm of "What's this?"

Widow Crockett They look like—they *are*. The children's sheets. (*Looking in a corner*) Look—"Simon"—(*Looking at a corner of the second sheet*) "Mary". I sewed their names on ... (*She is near to tears*)
Jack-in-the-Box They'll be all right.
Ragdoll They'll be all right.

Clockwork Panda growls an echo, "They'll be all right"

Widow Crockett Yes, of course. Come on, toys, let's start searching again. Come on, Arthur.

Arthur does not move

Come on. Mmm. Anyone got a carrot? Arthur. Oh dear, he's too upset to move. I know, we'll have to entertain him—make him laugh. Er—what do you call a donkey with a sore throat?
Jack-in-the-Box ⎫
Ragdoll ⎬ We don't know, what do you call a donkey ⎰ *speaking*
Clockwork Panda ⎭ with a sore throat? ⎱ *together*
Widow Crockett A little hoarse! Got it? Horse, hoarse—sore throat—ha ha ha ha! (*She encourages the Toys to laugh too*)

Arthur does not react

Oh, never mind. What do you call a donkey that's noisy and smelly?
Jack-in-the-Box ⎫
Ragdoll ⎬ We don't know, what do you call a donkey ⎰ *speaking*
Clockwork Panda ⎭ that's noisy and smelly? ⎱ *together*
Widow Crockett Winnie the Pooh! Get it? Whinny (*She makes the noise*)—the Pooh (*She holds her nose*) Noisy, smelly.

No reaction from Arthur

(*To the Toys*) I can't raise a smile, let alone a snigger. You have a go.

Two or three short "tricks" from the Toys follow. If possible, Jack-in-the-Box bounces and does an impressive somersault. Ragdoll does something floppily acrobatic or a contortion. Clockwork Panda does the "Da-Daaa" fanfare after each one. No reaction from Arthur

Ooh he's far gone, he really is. I know. Last try. We'll all—(*Taking in the audience*)—teach him a special dance. Arthur, you've heard of a fox-trot?

Arthur nods

This is the donkey trot! Come on, everyone, follow me.

SONG 10 **The Donkey Trot**

The song is accompanied by orchestrated actions

> Toss your head in the air with pride
> Wag your tail from side to side
> Stamp your hoof with a clip, clip, clop
> Have a good shake from bottom to top
> Now wiggle and jiggle and wriggle your ears
> Give it everything you've got
> Finally bray, hee haw, hee haw
> And you've danced the donkey trot.

The music continues

(*speaking*) Right, everyone, have a go.

All do the actions, leading the Audience. This is the equivalent of a songsheet. If desired, a songsheet could be lowered, or produced in some odd way. During this chorus, Arthur shows some interest

All   Toss your head in the air with pride
> Wag your tail from side to side
> Stamp your hoof with a clip, clip, clop
> Have a good shake from bottom to top
> Now wiggle and jiggle and wriggle your ears
> Give it everything you've got
> Finally bray, hee haw, hee haw
> And you've danced the donkey trot.

Widow Crockett Arthur's nearly doing it! Once more—everyone!

The chorus is repeated as required

During the song, if necessary, a front-cloth may be lowered in order to set the following scene; at the end of the song the Lights fade to a BLACKOUT

SCENE 2

The Glade of the Walking Trees

Another part of the wood. It will need to be set fairly far downstage to accommo-date the set for the transformation in the next scene; maybe a gauze, on which

are a number of trees. In front, prominent, are two trees, three-dimensional—all white like the rest of the wood

Pick and Nick enter, breathless; Nick carries the sack.

Nick (*demonstrating that the sack is heavy*) Ooooh. (*He drops the sack*)
Pick (*crossly*) Have you dropped the loot?
Nick No. Well, only a teeny weeny drop.
Pick Well, stop it. If you drop it you cop it. Got it?

Nick nods

This sack, it's worth packets. But we can't cash it if you bash it and smash it and crash it—dash it.
Nick But it's heavy. It's given my neck a crick, Pick! I heard it click, Pick!

Nick demonstrates—head on one side, plus a funny limping walk, to a percussion accompaniment

Pick Oh, poor old Nick. Just relax. Pick'll fix it!

Pick takes Nick's head and twists it—accompanied by a ratchet noise. It ends up on the other side. Nick does another funny walk, limping on the other foot

Nick That's even worse!
Pick Sorry. Split the difference!

He wrenches Nick's head again. This time it seems to vanish between Nick's shoulders, chin pressed in to chest. Nick does another funny walk. Pick sees it is wrong and tries again—he lifts the head up, accompanied by a cork popping noise

Nick Thanks, Pick. That's better. (*He goes to pick up the sack*)
Oh, I'm fed up with this wood going on and on and on.
Pick And I'm fed up with *you* going on and on and on.
Nick Can't we just hide the sack and come back for it, Pick?
Pick No.
Nick Why not?
Pick Why not? Because—(*Indicating the Audience*)—this lot of tell-tale-tits will sneak and grass to those two brats.
Nick What two brats?
Pick Those two brats who pretended to be ghosts and tried to scare us. They'll pay for that.
Nick } Oh yes.
Pick }
Pick They'd better look out.
Nick } Oh yes.
Pick }
Pick They'd . . .

Voices off make him stop—the Children calling "Arthur"

Here they come.
Nick Oh no!
Pick Quick, Nick. Ropes. We'll fix 'em.

Pick speedily unravels a rope from around his waist. Nick does the same. The Children's voices get nearer. Nick's trousers fall down. The two Robbers dash— in fact Nick hobbles—behind the two trees, one tree each. Nick suddenly remembers the sack and pops out again: But it is too late

Simple Simon and Contrary Mary enter

Nick retreats

Simple Simon }
Contrary Mary } Arthur, Arthur, where are you? etc. { *Calling together*

Contrary Mary suddenly spots the sack

Contrary Mary Simon, look! Father Christmas's toys. We've found them!

They start looking in the sack

Simple Simon Are they all there?

Sinister music, as the Robbers emerge from behind the trees. The Audience will doubtless warn the Children, who, for the moment remain absorbed in the sack. The Robbers hold the outstretched ropes above their heads. The Children suddenly become aware of the threat. They turn, see the Robbers, and dash between their legs, stop, turn and kick the Robbers up the backside. Each Child runs to one of the trees, pursued by a Robber

A choreographed chase follows. Suggested framework:
They chase round the trees once. Stop. Round the trees again. Stop. Round in the opposite direction. Stop. Cat and mouse side-stepping—from side to side with the tree-trunk between cat and mouse. Stop. Children concealed behind tree. Robbers start tip-toeing round; Children emerge going round in same direction and call "Yoo-hoo"! All about turn and chase round the trees again. Then the Robbers drop out of the chase—stand away from the trees. The Children go on round, thinking the Robbers are chasing them. Suddenly the Robbers pounce, using their ropes as lassoes to catch the Children. The Children struggle

Pick Tie them to the trees. We'll leave them here to ROT!

They push the Children up against the trees, and start to run round the trees in order to tie the Children to them. This they do, heads down, at some speed— if possible together in an almost stylized fashion. In their concentration, they fail to notice that the trees move—away from the Children, towards the centre— i.e. towards each other. So the Robbers only succeed in tying the ropes round the Children, not the trees as well. Unaware of this, they meet C and shake hands in triumph. They turn confidently to leave—upstage—and bump into the trees. The Robbers fall over, stand up, mystified, and are knocked over again by the trees which now advance, one on each Robber and chase them off. Nick just manages to grab the sack of toys on his way out

  Nick and Pick exit

The Children unravel themselves as the trees return to their original places

Contrary Mary This Magic Wood is fantastic! Ghosts, walking trees ...
Simple Simon I don't like it. It's too magic for me.

A door in each tree suddenly opens and Superwitch and Supermog step out

(*Gasping*) Look!

The Children react amazed, as the super pair step forward. Music continues throughout the scene

Superwitch Welcome, Simon. Welcome, Mary.
Simple Simon Who are you?
Contrary Mary (*excitedly*) A witch!
Superwitch Not *a* witch, Mary. I am Superwitch.

Short fanfare

(*Pointing*) Supermog, my cat.

During the above Supermog has yawned and stretched, and is now about to go to sleep

Supermog. This is no time for a supersnooze.

Supermog tries to stay awake

And this is my Magic Wood.
Simple Simon Well, that's all very nice but I think we ought to be off now.
Superwitch Wait! Wouldn't you like me to reveal to you more secrets of the Magic Wood?
Simple Simon Well ...
Contrary Mary Yes, please!
Simple Simon Mary!
Contrary Mary Well, I would. I've never met a real witch before, let alone a Superwitch.
Superwitch Supersplendid! Stand here. And watch and wonder.

SONG 11 **Superwitch's Super Spell**

Waving her broomstick, Superwitch chants her spell

> Broomstick, broomstick, hear my magic spell
> Show the children where I dwell.

(*speaking*) Superabrasupercadabra!

As the spell ends, the Light changes in dramatic fashion, with a magical sound effect. Possibly using a gauze, as described earlier, the next Scene is "mixed through"

SCENE 3

Superwitch's Supercottage

The cottage is all white, shaped like a witch's hat, with smoke coming from the top of the cone. There are two windows with window-boxes, and a door

Contrary Mary It's beautiful!

Simple Simon Hmm. Yes. Thanks, er—Superwitch. (*wanting to leave*) Come on, Mary, let's ...

Superwitch What is your favourite colour, Mary?

Contrary Mary Er—blue actually, and I like pink.

Superwitch Watch and wonder.

Superwitch points with her broomstick. Music echoes each movement—one by one flowers appear magically in the window boxes—blue and pink. Contrary Mary gasps and claps—she is completely won over by the excitement of it all

Are you hungry?

Contrary Mary Starving.

Superwitch (*meaningfully, but not too much*) So am I. What are your favourite things to eat?

Contrary Mary Er—lollipops.

Superwitch Watch and wonder.

Simple Simon Well, it's very kind of you, but ...

Contrary Mary Shhhh.

Superwitch points with her broomstick again. A flash. A lollipop tree magically appears

(*With a gasp*) A lollipop tree!

Superwitch Help yourselves.

The two Children, Simple Simon rather reluctantly, go to the tree and take a lollipop each

Contrary Mary It's like a dream!

Superwitch A Superdream! Now then, my dears, come inside if you wish.

Supermog opens the door and miaows politely, bowing

Contrary Mary Yes, please.

Simple Simon But, Mary ...

Contrary Mary What?

Simple Simon We ought to be getting home. Mother will be ...

Contrary Mary We won't stay for long. Don't be a spoilsport.

Superwitch Enter.

Simple Simon But ...

The Audience may shout a warning, but Contrary Mary grabs Simple Simon's hand and confidently walks in with him

Oh, all right.

Immediately, Supermog slams the door. Superwitch cackles with delight

Superwitch Superlative! Got you, my dears, my tasty little dears!

SONG 12 **I Love Children**

> I love children
> How I love the little children
> All those little dears are very dear to me
> They give such satisfaction

I love them to distraction
I love them for my breakfast, lunch and tea.

I love children
How I love the little children
Of the little things I couldn't have enough
I love them grilled or roasted
Or fried or poached or toasted
Except when they are overcooked and tough.

As people I admit I find them trying
They're noisy and they're naughty and they're rude
But one or maybe two—hot
In a casserole or stew-pot
Can really be remarkably good!

In the middle of the song, Superwitch magically points her broomstick at her cottage. It revolves, possibly helped by Supermog.

SCENE 4

Inside Superwitch's Supercottage

A white cauldron bubbles ominously. The song continues as Supermog grabs the Children firmly. They react uncertainly as Superwitch enters—still singing—and prods them and pinches them to test for cauldron-readiness

Superwitch   I love children
How I love the little children
Even though the little children don't love me
They're tasty and they're yummy
And when they're in my tummy
They're everything that they're cooked up to be!

Yes
I love children
How I love the little children

(To Contrary Mary and Simple Simon) I'm excited and delighted I've found you
You're both so very sweet
You look good enought to eat

(To the Audience) And that is what I now intend to do!

Just before the end of the song, she directs Supermog to draw back some curtains, revealing a cage. The Children, facing front, don't see this, till they are suddenly pushed smartly back and locked in the cage by Superwitch and Supermog. Superwitch cackles as she locks the door

Simple Simon What's going on?

Superwitch Your own, cosy little superroom, my dears. (*She deliberately gives Supermog the key*)

Contrary Mary But why are you locking us in?

Superwitch (*going to table/kitchen area*) To make supersure you don't miss the superfun!

Simple Simon Super fun?

Superwitch Now, my dears, eat. (*She hands them plates of goodies*) Delicious chestnut superpatties with bramble sauce. We've got to build you up. Superpatties make superfatties. Ha, ha. (*vehemently*) Eat.

The Children start eating

(*to Supermog*) Why is it we never find cauldron-ready children these days? They always need fattening up first. (*She cackles*) Now, (*to the Children*) Superwitch won't be long, my dears; I'm just going out to buy some supersage and onion stuffing.

Contrary Mary Where from?

Superwitch The Supermarket, of course!

Simple Simon I don't think I like supersage and onion stuffing.

Superwitch Really? (*Significantly, as she sets out her plate on the table, or better still, stirs the bubbling cauldron*) *I* do!

To a sinister chord, Superwitch exits, but immediately returns

Supermog—(*in an audible whisper*)—you're in charge. No falling asleep, understand? No catnapping on the job, If my supersupper escapes, I'll eat you instead ...

With a sotto voce cackle Superwitch exits, not forgetting to take her broomstick. Ideally she would fly off but this is not essential

Supermog deliberately places the key around his neck—it is on a string—and then goes to the cauldron, back to Audience, and starts throwing in herbs and spices and stirring them in. Simple Simon and Contrary Mary talk in whispers

Simple Simon (*frightened*) What are we going to do? She's going to eat us!

Contrary Mary (*testing the bars of the cage*) We've got to get out of here.

Simple Simon Yes. But how?

Contrary Mary makes a noise with the bars. Supermog swings round to check all is well. He makes a few threatening miaows and paw gestures, then returns to work. The Children react to this, by acting "good". They talk in whispers again

Contrary Mary We've got to get that key.

Simple Simon But it's round Supermog's neck.

Contrary Mary Exactly. Now, listen, what did Superwitch say to him just now?

Simple Simon I don't know—something about eating him if we escape ...

Contrary Mary No, before that—(*Taking in the Audience*)—anyone remember? I'm sure it could help.

She gleans from the Audience the information about Superwitch warning Supermog not to fall asleep

Of course! No catnaps. Supermog's always dropping off to sleep.
Simple Simon So?
Contrary Mary Let's help him drop off *now*!
Simple Simon How?
Contrary Mary Er—(*to the Audience*)—any ideas? (*With luck, she gets the idea of a lullaby from them*) Sing to him? Yes! A lullaby. Anyone know a good one? A good sending-off-to-sleep type song.

A song is selected from Audience suggestions. The most likely is "Rock-a-bye-baby". Having found one known by all or most of the Audience. Contrary Mary speaks

Right, let's "la la" it—very softly—or hum it!—Send him to sleep. After three. One, two, three.

The Children lead the very soft lullaby. After a few bars, Supermog reacts by yawning and stretching. Eventually, timing himself to the possibly different song each night, he curls up and goes into a deep sleep—in front of the Supercottage door

(*whispering*) Thank you! Well done.

Simple Simon stretches his hand and arm out of the bars but just fails to reach the key—which is visible, hanging from Supermog's neck

Stretch, stretch!
Simple Simon It's no good, I can't reach.

Contrary Mary and Simple Simon freeze as the lighting crossfades off the cottage interior either to one side of the stage or to a fairly visible part of the auditorium

Widow Crockett and the three Toys enter. The Toys see the Supercottage

Jack-in-the-Box Look!
Ragdoll Look!
Widow Crockett We've been looking for hours. We'll never find the children. We'll never see ...

By this time the Audience should be informing her that the Children are in the Supercottage

What? In there? In that overgrown upside down ice-cream cone?
Audience Yes.
Widow Crockett What are they doing in there?

She gleans the information that the Children have been locked in a cage in readiness to be eaten by Superwitch

That's terrible. What are we waiting for? Rescue party forward!

They all rush round the Supercottage, to reach the door. The lights come back up inside as Simple Simon struggles to get the key.

Simple Simon I've got it, I've got it!

Just as Simple Simon manages to get the key in his fingers, the door bursts open

Widow Crockett What's going on? I demand the release of my...

The door bangs into the sleeping Supermog, who wakes up and realizes something is up. He stretches

Contrary Mary Mother!
Widow Crockett Children! Have no fear, your mother's here!
Contrary Mary Go away!
Widow Crockett Go away? What a charming welcome! We've come to rescue you.
Contrary Mary Quick. Shut the door.

Widow Crockett enters and shuts the door as Supermog gets up and starts taking stock of what is going on

No! Get out!
Widow Crockett Eh? You said "Shut the door". I don't know. In, out, in, out, no gratitude the kids of today ... (*Muttering, she goes out again*)
Contrary Mary (*to the Audience*) Quick. A bit more lullaby. One, two, three.

Led by the Children, the Audience lullaby Supermog to sleep again—this time he is a little further from the door. By the end of the lullaby he is not fully asleep

Simple Simon (*having an idea*) He's still awake—yawn, everybody, yawn and stretch.

Led by the Children, the Audience yawn and stretch and send Supermog to sleep. Simple Simon nods off too

Contrary Mary That was a good idea, Simon. Simon!
Simple Simon (*waking with a start*) Ooh! They were so good, they got *me* nodding off too!

Widow Crockett pokes her head round the door

Widow Crockett (*whispering*) Can we creep in now?

The Children nod. Music, as Widow Crockett beckons the Toys inside. All keep as quiet as possible. After a brief mimed consultation between the Children and Widow Crockett, Clockwork Panda is called forward

Clockwork Panda, you're the key expert, it's up to you. Good luck.

Tension music, as Clockwork Panda approaches the sleeping Supermog. Ragdoll and Jack-in-the-Box watch from near the door. Widow Crockett stands farthest away from the cage. Clockwork Panda manages gently to remove the key from around Supermog's neck. He jerks his way to the cage, inserts the key in the lock, turns it to unlock the door, then uses the key as a doorknob to pull open the door, but, in doing so, the key comes out of the keyhole and Clockwork Panda drops it on the floor with a clatter. Instantaneously, Supermog wakes up, takes in what has happened, and springs ferociously at Clockwork Panda. Exciting music, as the two creatures stalk each other and fight. The others call out encouragement to Clockwork Panda. The Audience possibly will join in this

During the fight—stalkings, circlings, pounces, wrestling, etc., plus growlings and miaows, Jack-in-the-Box and Ragdoll edge their way to the cage and open

*the door. The fight nears this spot and in order to avoid being involved in this,
they nip inside the cage and help Contrary Mary and Simple Simon to get out.
Contrary Mary and Simple Simon edge their way round to Widow Crockett
and are reunited with her; but their joy is short-lived as regular grunts from
Clockwork Panda, accompanied by a jerky slowing up, tells everyone that his
clockwork is running down. All watch stunned, as he stops altogether. Supermog
continues making threatening gestures, as if to warn anyone thinking of helping
Clockwork Panda. Widow Crockett attempts to reach Clockwork Panda, just
grabs his key and is about to turn it when Supermog pounces and forces Widow
Crockett away, back to the two Children. Supermog triumphantly pushes Clockwork Panda over; he lies helplessly inert on the floor. Supermog springs to the
cage, picks up the key, and before the stunned Ragdoll and Jack-in-the-Box can
react and get out of the cage, Supermog has locked the door on them. Supermog
does not realize the Children have escaped—he assumes that Ragdoll and Jack-
in-the-Box are the two children. Supermog replaces the key round his neck*

*Sudden cackle noises off tell everyone that Superwitch is back. Feverish activity
in the Supercottage. Supermog drags Clockwork Panda out of the main view,
then returns to work at the cauldron. Widow Crockett and the Children do their
best to hide in the cage area, behind the curtains. N.B. Supermog is unaware
of Widow Crockett's presence*

Superwitch enters, with her broomstick: ideally, she flies in on it

Superwitch They'd run out of supersausage and onion. I had to get supersausage and prune stuffing instead. Now then. Supercauldron bubbling and
boiling?

Supermog miaows

Supersplendid.

*Superwitch goes to the cage. Jack-in-the-Box and Ragdoll turn away, backs
to her, as she approaches*

A pinch and a prod
Before heating
Just make sure
They're ripe for eating.

She prods and pinches Jack-in-the-Box through the bars

My word, Simon, you're all hard and bony. No fat. No *flesh.*

She tries Ragdoll

And Mary! You're all soft and flabby. No bone. What strange children
you are. Never mind. The supercauldron is prepared and Superwitch is
superhungry. Come, my dears, time to take a dip—the water's lovely and
warm. Ha, ha, ha. Supermog, the key.

*Dramatic tension music, as Supermog opens the door, using the key. He leaves
it in the lock, then enters the cage and picks up Jack-in-the-Box, from behind.
He waits. Superwitch enters the cage and picks up Ragdoll, from behind. To
do this, she puts down her broomstick, inside the cage. They lift them out of the
cage and start to cross to the cauldron. The tension increases. Suddenly, Jack-*

in-the-Box starts bouncing—springing right out of Supermog's grasp. Simulta-neously, Ragdoll goes all floppy and slides through Superwitch's arms into a heap on the floor

There follows a short section in which the two "Supers" attempt to lift the two Toys and put them in the cauldron. But every time they are foiled by the strong springy bounces of Jack-in-the-Box and the rubbery contortions of Ragdoll. The sequence should use as much acrobatic ability as the two Toys can muster. Fin-ally, the two Toys dash back to the cage and get inside. Superwitch and Supermog follow—into the cage. They grab the Toys—who suddenly get away with such speed they can get out of the cage and shut the door. Widow Crockett rushes out of hiding and turns the key. The Children follow. Cheers of triumph

Widow Crockett You crafty old conniving cannibal lady, you. I'll teach you to take advantage of my poor children.

With musical accompaniment, Widow Crockett passes, very deliberately, the key down the line of Children and Toys. The final one drops it into the cauldron. Superwitch and Supermog scrabble at the bars of the cage, furious

See how *you* like being locked up!

Contrary Mary rewinds Clockwork Panda. So all six—Children and rescue party—are lined up triumphantly viewing the caged fallen superpowers

Superwitch You'll pay for this, you interfering old beanbag.
Widow Crockett Sticks and stones may break my bones, but words will never hurt me.
Simple Simon They will if a dictionary falls on your head.
Widow Crockett Quiet, Simon.
Superwitch You meddling old maggotface...
Widow Crockett Hold your tongue and take your medicine. (*To the others*) Rescuers and rescued, ready? Home.

She starts to lead them out

Superwitch (*vehemently*) You will *never* go home. (*Producing her broomstick which starts to pulsate*) Superwitch rules!

SONG 12A **Superwitch's Super Spell** (*reprise*)

All stiffen zombie-like as the broomstick is pointed at them

> Broomstick, broomstick, hear my magic plea
> Find a way to set me free.

(*Speaking*)   Superabrasupercadabra.

As the spell ends, Superwitch points the broomstick at the cauldron. Eerie music and lighting changes to focus on the key of the cage, rising mysteriously from the cauldron untouched by human hand! Strong "invisible" nylon thread from above may best effect this. It gently flies past the helpless Widow Crockett and company and lands at the cage. Supermog puts his hand through the bars, collects the key and unlocks the cage door. Superwitch and Supermog make their escape. Then Superwitch points the broomstick at Widow Crockett and company.

Mechanically all six of them start moving in time, controlled by Superwitch, into the cage. Music echoes this. Supermog locks the door. The lighting returns to normal. Widow Crockett and company "wake up" to find themselves locked in. Superwitch cackles with self-congratulation. Supermog hangs up the key

Superwitch rules!

Short celebratory fanfare

Widow Crockett (*temporarily confused*) But—where—how did you do that?
Simple Simon Magic, Mother.
Contrary Mary The magic broomstick.
Superwitch Exactly, my dears. (*Moving to the cauldron*) And now Superwitch's supertummy is rumbling. I am hungry, my dears. And you know what that means. The cauldron is still bubbling and boiling, my dears.

Tension music

Supermog—bring the children here.

Widow Crockett and company are alarmed, as Supermog approaches the cage

Widow Crockett (*desperately trying to think of something to do*) Wait!
Superwitch I have waited long enough, thanks to your interference.
Widow Crockett Yes, yes—I'm sorry—it was stupid, impulsive—you won easily—we mortals could never expect to get the better of ...
Superwitch A Superwitch? Exactly.
Widow Crockett You must do with us as you will.
Contrary Mary Mother!
Simple Simon You can't give in now! She's going to sizzle us for supper!
Widow Crockett I'm sorry, Children. Ordinary folk like us can do nothing to overcome a Superpower.
Superwitch (*flattered*) You are intelligent. At first I estimated you had less brain than a stuffed olive.
Widow Crockett Oh. Thank you. But, you know, nothing you have done so far—however magical and impressive—has actually—if you'll forgive me saying so—convinced me that you are a *real* witch ...
Superwitch Careful, old face-like-a-wrinkled-prune ...
Widow Crockett No, no, please let me finish—you probably *are* a real witch, but—
Superwitch (*angrily*) Probably?
Widow Crockett —but when I was small, all the *real* witches in the books I read could do one thing that—well—forgive me but—well—one thing that I don't think you can do ...

Pause

Superwitch (*breathing heavily*) And what, may I ask, was that?
Widow Crockett They could, by magic, turn themselves into something else— *anything* else.
Superwitch I can do that. How dare you suggest Superwitch cannot turn herself into something else—*anything* else.
Widow Crockett Then prove it.

Superwitch What?
Widow Crockett Please.

SONG 13 **Prove To Us You're A Witch**

Widow Crockett   Prove to us you're a witch

Superwitch (*Speaking*) I *am* a witch.

Widow Crockett   I challenge you to live up to your name
Prove to us you're a witch

Superwitch (*speaking*) Superwitch!

Widow Crockett   Prove your power is as potent as you claim.

After a pause—tension music

Superwitch Very well. Supermog, hold the broomstick. (*She composes herself*) Superwitch is ready.
Widow Crockett Turn yourself into—a dog.
Superwitch (*closing her eyes and mumbling*) Ickerbya, dickerbya, one, two, three.

Noise. Flash. As quickly as possible the transformation is revealed—where Superwitch stood, there is now a white dog. Supermog still stands brandishing the broomstick. Widow Crockett and company applaud, impressed. Supermog miaows, frightened of the dog, and runs to hide

(*Voice only—from the dog area if possible*) Supermog, don't be silly, it's only me. I won't hurt you.

Supermog relaxes

Hold out the broomstick.

Supermog does so

Dickerbya, ickerbya, three, two, one.

Noise. Flash. The dog disappears and Superwitch is back. Widow Crockett and company applaud. Superwitch beams with pride

Widow Crockett Wonderful.
Superwitch Thank you. (*Going to the cauldron*) Supermog, get the children. I'm starving.
Widow Crockett Oh—oh, please—one more demonstration. Then I will apologize to you for ever having doubted your superpowers.
Contrary Mary So will I!
Simple Simon So will I!
Jack-in-the-Box So will I!
Ragdoll So will I!

Clockwork Panda gives three long grunts

Widow Crockett (*taking in Audience*) We *all* will, won't we?
Audience Yes!

SONG 13A **Prove To Us You're A Witch** (*reprise*)

Widow Crockett
Simple Simon
Contrary Mary
Jack-in-the-Box   } (*singing*)   Prove to us you're a witch
Ragdoll
(Clockwork Panda)

Superwitch (*with intense concentration*) I am a witch.

The Others   We challenge you to live up to your name
                                Prove to us you're a witch

Superwitch   Superwitch!

The Others   Prove your power is as potent as you
                                claim.

Superwitch Very well, but this is the last time. (*She composes herself*) Superwitch is ready.

Widow Crockett Turn yourself into a—*mouse*.

Superwitch (*closing her eyes and mumbling*) Ockerbya, dockerbya, one, two,
three.

*Noise. Flash. Superwitch turns into a tiny white mouse—perhaps a clockwork
one. Widow Crockett and company applaud and cheer*

Widow Crockett (*quietly*) Supermog, look—a mouse.

*Dramatic chord as Supermog, delighted, sees the mouse, drops the broomstick
and springs to the attack, playing with the mouse, tossing it about, etc., etc.*

Superwitch (*voice over, as though coming from the mouse*) No, no. Supermog.
It's me, you stupid cat. Superwitch. Help! Stop it! Stop! Help! etc., etc.

*Widow Crockett and company shout encouragement to Supermog. The Audience
may well join in. Finally, Supermog kills the mouse—and eats it. Cheers*

Widow Crockett Well done, Supermog. (*To the others*) I've heard of the biter
bit—that was the eater eaten!

Contrary Mary Supermog, there are lots more mice in the Magic Wood—
and you're free now!

Supermog looks happy, and runs out of the Supercottage with excitement

Cheers

Thank you for saving us, Mother.

Simple Simon And the toys. Thanks.

Jack-in-the-Box A pleasure.

Ragdoll A pleasure.

Clockwork Panda grunts

Widow Crockett Quiet! Delightful though all these thank-yous and don't-
mention-its may be, you seem to forget one rather vital thing.

All What?
Widow Crockett (*screaming*) We're still locked in this rotten old cage!

Glum faces return

And there's no-one who can let us out!

The action freezes as the lights crossfade to another area—the side of the stage from which the Widow and company entered last

Music as Arthur, the Donkey, enters, searching for the others. He looks, shakes his head, then looks again

The Audience will probably immediately shout out "they're in the cottage", or "in the cage". If so, Arthur takes instructions from the Audience, being led by them round to the front door. If no Audience reaction comes, he finds his way round anyway and Widow Crockett and company hear him and call out "Arthur". Then the lights go up again inside the Supercottage, and Arthur enters. All react joyfully: "Arthur!", "Hallo", etc., etc.

Arthur, dear, can you get us out of this mess?

Arthur looks at the situation, then tries a couple of backward kicks to break the lock on the door: but these attempts fail

Contrary Mary The key, Arthur, find the key.

Arthur looks bemused

Simple Simon Where is it?

The Audience will probably lead Arthur to it. If not, Contrary Mary remembers where it is and directs Arthur towards it. N.B. It is still where Supermog left it earlier. Arthur gets the key—either in his mouth or by knocking it to the floor and then kicking it to the cage

Widow Crockett Well done, Arthur.

Music, as Widow Crockett opens the cage door and all file out. As the first in the line reaches the Superdoor—it bursts open, taking everyone by surprise.

Pick and Nick enter with the sack of toys

Pick (*seeing Arthur*) There you are, you evil equine escaper. Come here. (*He goes to Arthur*)

Nick sees Widow Crockett and company

Nick (*nervously*) Pick ...
Pick I'll beat the liv ...
Nick Pick. *Pick!*
Pick What?
Nick Those kids what we left to rot.
Pick What about them?
Nick They haven't rotted yet.
Pick What?

He turns to see the others. The six are closing in on the Robbers

Oh. Ah. Now look—quick, Nick, run!

Contrary Mary and Simple Simon pick up the broomstick and point it at the Robbers who immediately stop, frozen. Nick drops the sack of toys

SONG 13B **Superwitch's Super Spell** (*reprise*)

Contrary Mary ⎫   Broomstick, broomstick, hear our magic song
Simple Simon ⎭   Put those thieves where they belong.

Both take a deep breath to intone the magic word, but stop, horror-stricken

Contrary Mary (*speaking*) What was it? The magic word?
Simple Simon (*speaking*) I've forgotten it!
Contrary Mary (*to the Audience*) Anyone remember it?
Audience Superabrasupercadabra!
Contrary Mary ⎫ Thank you. (*Intoning the magic word*) Super- ⎰ *Speaking*
Simple Simon ⎭ abrasupercadabra!   ⎱ *together*

As the spell ends Contrary Mary and Simple Simon "magic" the Robbers into the cage; they walk mechanically and zombie-like. Clockwork Panda turns the key and locks them in, then Jack-in-the-Box bounces over and throws the key in the cauldron. Contrary Mary and Simple Simon rush to the sack to check everything is there. Pick and Nick "wake up"

Nick ⎫ Mercy, mercy. ⎰ *Speaking*
Pick ⎭   ⎱ *together*
Widow Crockett Qui—et. We're leaving you to rot, you rotten lot. So have the decency to rot quietly. With dignity. Right. Home, everyone.
Simple Simon How?
Widow Crockett Back through the Magic Wood, I suppose.
Contrary Mary Couldn't we use this? (*Indicating the broomstick*)
Widow Crockett What, fly?
Contrary Mary Why not?
Widow Crockett We'd never all fit on.
Contrary Mary No, look—all hold hands.

They all come forward, allowing the gauze to fly back in. All including Arthur, hold on to one another. At the front is Widow Crockett

Mother, you climb aboard.

Widow Crockett gets on the broomstick

And all sing the superspell.

SONG 13C **Superwitch's Super Spell** (*reprise*)

Widow Crockett ⎫
Contrary Mary ⎪
Simple Simon ⎪   Broomstick, broomstick, hear our magic rhyme
Jack-in-the-Box ⎬   Help us through the air to climb.
Ragdoll ⎪
(Clockwork Panda) ⎭

They encourage the Audience to join in the magic word

(*Speaking*) Superabrasupercadabra!

During and after the spell, the scene changes

Scene 5

The Sky

It is suggested that the gauze flies in behind the characters and that dry ice be used to suggest clouds. Maybe projection onto the gauze can suggest a moving sky

To exciting music Widow Crockett and company appear to be flying—all six, and Arthur. After a short time they exit

Then if possible there is a change to a U.V. section, in which cut-out pictures of the Flying procession are moved across in front of blacks. Maybe a second smaller set of cut-outs returns in the other direction, or silhouette shapes could be used. N.B. This section can be done in several different ways. The important thing is to provide an exciting visual piece of action in the sky—while at the same time allowing time for the scene change behind.

Scene 6

Inside Widow Crockett's Toyshop. Night

Everything is now back to "reality". When the Lights go up, the picture is exactly as it was in Act I Scene 2, when Widow Crockett and the Children went to sleep at their benches. They are all back in their first costumes. The only difference is that the pile of finished toys, ready to be collected by Father Christmas, is on the bench. The main point to be established now, and during the scene, is that all that has happened since they went to sleep has been a dream

Music for atmosphere, as Father Christmas comes down the chimney. He brushes himself off, looks around, sees his mince pie waiting for him, smiles and eats it. Then he quietly creeps over to the sleeping Widow Crockett and gently wakes her up

Widow Crockett (*still half-asleep*) Oooh, I ache all over. I'll never use a broomstick for a long journey again—even a magic one. I ... (*Waking, she sees Father Christmas*). Aaaaah! Red Riding Hood's grown a beard ...
Father Christmas It's all right, Widow Crockett, it's only me.
Widow Crockett Father Christmas!
Father Christmas My annual visit.
Widow Crockett I'm sorry. I've just had the most extra-out-of-the-ordinary dream ... (*Realizing, looking at alarm clock, she gasps*) We've slept through the alarm! Oh no! Father Christmas, for the first time Widow Crockett and Daughter and Son have failed you—we haven't finished your order. Simon, Mary, wake up! We've all overslept.

Simon and Mary wake up

Say sorry to Father Christmas.

Simple Simon (*yawning*) Sorry ... (*Excitedly*) Father Christmas?

Father Christmas Hallo, Simon. Hallo, Mary.

Contrary Mary Are you the *real* Father Christmas?

Widow Crockett Mary, don't be contrary.

Father Christmas (*laughing*) Of course I am, pull my beard if you like!

Simple Simon Did you find the ...

Father Christmas The mince pie was delicious. Thank you.

Contrary Mary It *is* Father Christmas.

Widow Crockett Of course it is—and we've failed him.

Father Christmas But ...

Widow Crockett He'll never ask us to make toys for him again.

Father Christmas (*spotting the toys*) But ...

Widow Crockett He'll take away our "By appointment to" sign and we'll be disgraced. (*She sobs violently*)

The Children comfort her

Father Christmas But *look*! Aren't those toys for me?

Silence. Pause. All look

They look finished all right.

Wide-eyed, Widow Crockett and the Children go to the finished toys

Widow Crockett
Simple Simon
Contrary Mary
(*Suddenly, to one another, in awed unison*) Are you thinking what I'm thinking? Jack-in-the-Box, Ragdoll, Clockwork Panda? Did you dream that *they* finished Father Christmas's order? Yes. But they couldn't have. Well, *someone* has. And it wasn't one of you? No. Well then...? (*With a sudden thought*) What else was in your dream? The Magic Wood? Yes. Superwitch? Yes, Supermog? Yes. Phew! *Speaking together*

Widow Crockett (*changing gear*) Sorry, Father Christmas—great minds thinking alike!

Father Christmas Well, clearly something mysterious and magical has happened here tonight—and it couldn't have happened to a nicer family. (*He loads his toys—probably by gathering up the sheet on which the toys are lying*) I must be off. The reindeer's got a gammy leg and we're getting behind. Happy Christmas, everyone! (*He goes to the chimney and is about to climb up*)

Widow Crockett
Simple Simon
Contrary Mary
Good-bye, Father Christmas, see you next year, etc. *Speaking together*

Suddenly the door flies open, having been kicked by Pick and Nick, who storm in, taking everyone by surprise

Pick Right. Do as you're told and no-one'll get hurt.

Widow Crockett It's the furniture removers. This time you can remove yourselves.

Pick We want our donkey back.

Nick Please.

Simple Simon How did you get out of the cage?

Pick What?

Simple Simon We locked you in Superwitch's cage.

Nick Eh?

Contrary Mary No we didn't, Simon—that was all in our dream. We dreamed it.

Pick Well, *we* didn't dream *anything*.

Nick No, you tricked Pick and Nick and nicked it.

Widow Crockett I beg your pardon?

Pick The donkey. Where is it?

At this moment Arthur the Donkey enters, knocking Pick and Nick flying

Nick Hey!

Pick You ...

They get up but Arthur gives them each a back kick and floors them again

Widow Crockett Now get out.

Pick ⎫ It's *our* donkey ...

Nick ⎪ It's not fair ...

Simple Simon ⎬ If you can't look after a donkey properly, ⎰ *Speaking*
              ⎪ you ...   ⎱ *together*

Contrary Mary ⎪ We're taking care of him ...

Widow Crockett ⎭ Get out, get out ...

Father Christmas steps back into the scene

Father Christmas Hey! Stop it! Stop arguing! Qui-et!

All stop in surprise

Nick (*to Pick*) Gosh, Pick, it's Father Christmas!

Pick So it is. It's the real Old Nick, Nick.

Father Christmas This won't do. All this squabbling. It's the season of good-will and happiness, when you should all bury the hatchet and be friends!

     ⎫ That's all very well ...

All ⎬ Yes, but ...   ⎰ *Speaking*

     ⎭ You don't understand, etc., etc.   ⎱ *together*

Father Christmas Hush.

All are quiet again

From what I've heard—(*To the Children*)—you stole their donkey; that's serious—

Simple Simon and Contrary Mary look sheepish

—but (*To the Robbers*), you ill-treated the donkey—

Pick and Nick look sheepish

—that's even more serious. I have a suggestion. If—(*To the Robbers*)—you let the donkey stay here to be looked after properly—I'll give you a very special Christmas present.

Pause

Pick All right, then.

Nick (*excitedly*) I said we might get a present!

Father Christmas (*to the Children*) Now then. The donkey can stay here—

Contrary Mary ⎫ Thank you. ⎰ *Speaking*
Simple Simon ⎭ ⎱ *together*

Father Christmas —on one condition.

Contrary Mary What's that?

Father Christmas That you allow him to come and work for me on Christmas Eve. I told you my reindeer's got a gammy leg. Your donkey—what's his name, by the way?

Simple Simon Arthur.

Father Christmas Arthur can pull my sleigh!

Cheers. Arthur paws the ground appreciatively, and nods his head. Arthur and the two Robbers shake hands with Simple Simon and Contrary Mary, then Father Christmas gives the Robbers a present. Widow Crockett comes forward

Music starts under the dialogue

Widow Crockett Children!

The Children come forward

Contrary Mary Yes, Mother?

Widow Crockett Everything seems to have worked out all right, eh?

Simple Simon Yes.

Widow Crockett Are you *sure* you two didn't finish off Father Christmas's order?

Simple Simon Sure.

Contrary Mary Really.

Widow Crockett (*shaking her head*) It looks as though I'm going to have to believe in Fairy Godmothers now—doesn't it? (*She smiles and hugs the delighted Children*)

SONG 13D **If Only** (*reprise*)

During the song, Father Christmas climbs up the chimney, and all the others wave good-bye

Widow Crockett
(*accompanied by
Simple Simon and
Contrary Mary
singing to "Ah"*)

If only
There was such a thing as magic
Just think of all the wondrous spells we'd weave
Maybe the impossible we only dream about
Could be possible
If only
We'd believe.

And the fantasies we make up
Might be real when we wake up

All

If only
We'd just believe.

All leave the toyshop to wave good-bye to Father Christmas. If they remain visible to the audience, they freeze

The music continues, changing to the "toys" theme, as the action freezes, and the lights change. On the workbench inside the toyshop the bag of magic conkers lights up and pulsates. The box flies open and Jack-in-the-Box pops up. He goes and "wakes" Ragdoll then together they wind up Clockwork Panda. They all shake hands, happy at the outcome of the story. They almost wink at the audience and put a finger to their mouths, as though to say "We did finish Father Christmas's orders but don't tell anyone—it's our secret!"

As though from nowhere the Fairy Godmother suddenly becomes visible downstage smiling contentedly, happy that her mission was successful

SONG 13E **Toys** (*reprise*)

Jack-in-the-Box ⎤	Toys
Ragdoll ⎟	Keep you company
(Clockwork Panda) ⎬	When you're all at sea
Fairy Godmother ⎦	When you need a friend
	For sure your
	Toys
	Never let you down
	Always stick
	Around
	Till there's a happy end.

The Toys gradually slow down and revert to their lifeless state, as—

The CURTAIN *falls*

FINALE

Probably singing "By Appointment to Father Christmas", the cast enter to take their calls. If possible, the toyshop can be revolved so that the Crockett family can enter from it
As a climax to the song and curtain calls, snow falls, and the cast divide to welcome Father Christmas on his sleigh—drawn by Arthur the Donkey

SONG 13F **If Only** (*reprise*)

All   (*after singing the first part to "Ah"*)
          And the fantasies we make up
          Could be real when we wake up
          If only
          We'd just believe.

CURTAIN

As a final reprise, it is suggested that Widow Crockett leads the cast, and the Audience, in a full version—with movements and words, and Arthur's dance—of THE DONKEY TROT

FINAL CURTAIN

FURNITURE AND PROPERTY LIST

PROLOGUE

On stage: Grassy tuffet
Picnic basket

Personal: **Fairy Godmother:** wand

ACT I

Scene 1

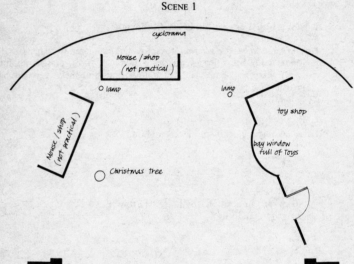

On stage: Lamps, Christmas tree
Lantern for CAROL SINGERS
In Toyshop: various toys and parcels

Off stage: Bag of "white conkers" (**Fairy Godmother**)
Rope (**Nick**)
Stick (**attached to Donkey**)
Saddle-bag with picnic materials, sandwiches (**Donkey**)
Toy swords (**Simple Simon, Contrary Mary**)

SCENE 2

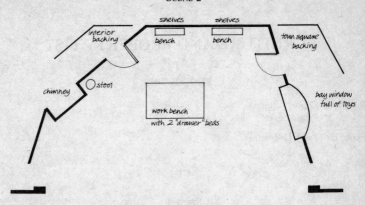

On stage: Rostrum with 2 drawer "beds" and bedding
          Work benches
          On shelves, benches and rostrum: toys, toy-making materials, bags of bal-
              loons, teddy bears, jigsaw puzzles, sandpaper, tools, pins, wrapping
              paper, fake spray-paint can, cloths, toy drums and sticks, toy musical
              instruments, etc.
          Skateboard
          Fancy apron
          Scroll-like list
          Large colourful clock with automatic bird
          Alarm clock

SCENE 3

On stage: As Act I Scene 1
          Donkey rope in position, toy horse tied to one end
          In Toyshop: handbell

SCENE 4

On stage: As Act I Scene 2

Off stage: Plate with mince pie (**Widow Crockett**)
           Sack (**"Father Christmas"—Nick**)

SCENE 5

On stage: One or two cut-out shapes—optional
          Hazard (stile or chasm with rope)—optional

SCENE 6

On stage: White trees, set to grow during Transformation

Off stage: White broomstick (**Superwitch**)

ACT II

SCENE 1

On stage: As close of Act I, but thicker trees and white log seat

Off stage: Song sheet—optional

SCENE 2

On stage: Gauze with trees
2 3-dimensional trees with doors

Off stage: 2 ropes (**Pick, Nick**)

SCENE 3

On stage: Cone-shaped cottage with smoke from roof
Trick window boxes
Trick lollipop tree

SCENE 4

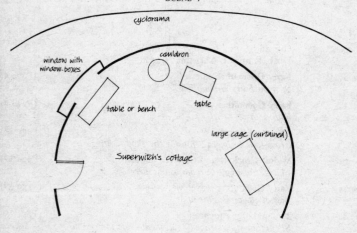

On stage: Bubbling cauldron with ladle, pots of herbs, spices, cooking materials
Large cage behind curtains; key on string in door
Table with plates of "goodies", etc.
White dog (concealed)
White mouse (concealed)

SCENE 5

On stage: Cut-out shapes—optional

SCENE 6

On stage: Everything as when **Widow Crockett** and **Children** went to sleep in Act
I Scene 2
Finished toys on sheet

Off stage: Sleigh (**Father Christmas**)

LIGHTING PLOT

The following plot may be elaborated according to the facilities available

Property fittings required: illuminated Christmas tree; street lamps

Various interior and exterior settings

PROLOGUE

To open:	Spots concentrated on downstage area; snow effect	
Cue 1:	**Contrary Mary**: "I don't want to go home" *Flash*	(Page 1)
Cue 2:	**Fairy Godmother** produces wand *Lights brighten: spot on FAIRY GODMOTHER*	(Page 2)

ACT I

To open:	Overall lighting to suggest Christmas scene. Dusk, lamps lit, Christmas tree lit	
Cue 3:	**Fairy Godmother** enters *Spot on Fairy Godmother*	(Page 4)
Cue 4:	**Fairy Godmother** exits *Fade spot*	(Page 4)
Cue 5:	At end of Scene 1 *Cross-fade to overall interior toy shop lighting*	(Page 14)
Cue 6:	**Widow Crockett** and **Children** fall asleep *Change to suggest dream atmosphere*	(Page 19)
Cue 7:	**Fairy Godmother** waves wand *Bag of conkers lights up*	(Page 19)
Cue 8:	Toy making sequence *Silent film-style strobe effect, then revert to previous lighting*	(Page 19)
Cue 9:	At end of Scene 2 *Fade to Black-out, then up to Town Square lighting— night but not dark. Lamps and Christmas tree lit*	(Page 24)
Cue 10:	At end of Scene 3 *Cross-fade to toyshop interior*	(Page 28)
Cue 11:	**Children** settle to sleep *Lamps and tree out—general dim of lighting*	(Page 28)
Cue 12:	As **Toys** wake up *Silent film-style strobe effect, returning to previous lighting*	(Page 33)
Cue 13:	At end of Scene 4 *Cross-fade to silhouette mime lighting*	(Page 33)
Cue 14:	At end of Scene 5 *Change to general moonlight effect*	(Page 34)

Cue 15:	**Robbers** throw conkers away *Strange pulsating light, increasing to dazzling white through Transformation*	(Page 36)
Cue 16:	**Children**: "We're lost! Help!" *Flash*	(Page 38)
Cue 17:	**Superwitch**: "Supermog!" *Flash*	(Page 39)

ACT II

To open:	Similar to close of Act I, with dark blue background	
Cue 18:	At end of Scene 1 *Fade to Black-out, then up to downstage Wood scene*	(Page 46)
Cue 19:	At end of **Superwitch**'s spell *Dramatic lighting change to Scene 3*	(Page 49)
Cue 20:	**Superwitch** produces Lollipop Tree *Flash*	(Page 50)
Cue 21:	At end of Scene 3 *Cross-fade to cottage interior*	(Page 51)
Cue 22:	**Simple Simon**: "I can't reach" *Cross-fade to exterior of cottage*	(Page 53)
Cue 23:	**Widow Crockett** goes to door *Cross-fade to interior of cottage*	(Page 53)
Cue 24:	**Superwitch** points broomstick at cauldron *Lighting shrinks to focus on key—return to normal as Supermog opens door*	(Page 56)
Cue 25:	**Superwitch**: "... one, two, three." *Flash*	(Page 58)
Cue 26:	**Superwitch**: "... three, two one." *Flash*	(Page 58)
Cue 27:	**Superwitch**: "... one, two, three." *Flash*	(Page 59)
Cue 28:	**Widow Crockett**: "... who can let us out!" *Cross-fade to exterior of cottage, return to previous lighting as Donkey enters cottage*	(Page 60)
Cue 29:	At end of Scene 4 *Cross-fade to Sky lighting, with U.V. light sequence—optional*	(Page 62)
Cue 30:	At end of Scene 5 *Cross-fade to lighting exactly as when Widow Crock- ett and Children went to sleep in Act I Scene 2— toyshop interior, night*	(Page 62)
Cue 31:	**Children** wave good-bye to Father Christmas *Change to "dream" lighting; magic conkers light up*	(Page 66)
Cue 32:	**Toys** shake hands *Bring up spot on Fairy Godmother*	(Page 66)
Cue 33:	As CURTAIN falls *Full up for Finale—snow effect*	(Page 66)

EFFECTS PLOT

ACT I

Cue 1:   **Contrary Mary**: "I don't want to go home"   (Page 1)
Loud noise

Cue 2:   Bag of conkers lights up   (Page 19)
Eerie electronic noise

Cue 3:   **Clockwork Panda** is wound up   (Page 19)
Ratchet noise—repeat

Cue 4:   At end of toy-making sequence   (Page 20)
Alarm clock goes off

Cue 5:   **Robbers** throw conkers away   (Page 36)
Eerie electronic sounds

ACT II

Cue 6:   After **Robbers** enter   (Page 41)
Owl hoots

Cue 7:   **Pick** twists **Nick**'s head   (Page 47)
Ratchet noise—repeat with business, change to cork-popping noise when Pick lifts Nick's head up

Cue 8:   As **Superwitch**'s spell ends   (Page 49)
Magical sound effect

Cue 9:   **Superwitch**: "... one two, three."   (Page 58)
Sharp noise

Cue 10:   **Superwitch**: "... three, two one."   (Page 58)
Sharp noise

Cue 11:   **Superwitch**: "... one, two, three."   (Page 59)
Sharp noise

Printed in Great Britain by Butler & Tanner Ltd, Frome and London